TEACHING CRIMINOLOGY AT THE INTERSECTION

Teaching about gender, race, social class and sexuality in criminal justice and criminology classrooms can be challenging. Professors may face resistance when they ask students to examine how gender impacts victimization, how race affects interactions with the police, how socioeconomic status shapes experiences in court or how sexuality influences treatment in the criminal justice system. *Teaching Criminology at the Intersection* is an instructional guide to support faculty as they navigate teaching these topics.

Bringing together the experience and knowledge of expert scholars, this book provides time-strapped academics with an accessible how-to guide for the classroom, where the dynamics of gender, race, class and sexuality demographics intersect and permeate criminal justice concerns. In the book, the authors of each chapter discuss how they teach a particular contemporary criminal justice issue and provide their suggestions for best practice, while grounding their ideas in pedagogical theory. Chapters end with a toolkit of recommended activities, assignments, films, readings or websites.

As a teaching handbook, *Teaching Criminology at the Intersection* is appropriate reading for graduate level criminology, criminal justice and women's and gender studies teaching instruction courses, and as background reading and reference for instructors in these disciplines.

Rebecca M. Hayes is an Associate Professor in the Department of Sociology, Anthropology and Social Work at Central Michigan University.

Kate Luther is an Assistant Professor of Sociology at Pacific Lutheran University.

Susan Caringella is a Professor of Sociology at Western Michigan University and an internationally known expert on rape, feminism and criminology.

"*Teaching Criminology at the Intersection* is something every faculty member needs who is struggling with how to address issues of inequality and discrimination to resistant or simply unknowledgeable students. The contributors use various techniques, such as drawing an analogy between inaccurate perceptions of American Pit Bull Terriers and racist beliefs about people of color, effective use of assignments and outside speakers, and classroom exercises to impart knowledge in a non-threatening and often experiential manner. In her ground-breaking chapter, Emily Lenning introduces students to the experiences of LGBTQ persons by having them imagine being heterosexual in a homosexist world. This book should be on the shelf of everyone who cares about teaching."

Susan F. Sharp, *David Ross Boyd Professor/Presidential Professor, University of Oklahoma, USA*

"It is vitally important that instructors teaching criminal justice broach the topic of diversity and its relationship to crime and criminal justice issues; however, incorporating material on race, ethnicity, gender, class, and sexual orientation can be a daunting task. Some of the most important topics to cover are the most sensitive, and instructors risk alienating students if the material is not approached carefully. This important book provides instructors with tools to tackle difficult issues and adequately address how diversity shapes human behavior, and encourages students to self-reflect on their own behavior and experiences."

Christina DeJong, *Director, Center for Integrative Studies in Social Science and Associate Professor, School of Criminal Justice, Michigan State University, USA*

"In their scrupulous consideration of the compelling effects of gender, race, class, and sexuality within criminology, the contributors of this volume have identified a missing link in the instruction of criminological courses.

This volume provides concrete illustrations for criminology educators to follow and promotes creative formulation of sound methods for educating from a critical and inclusivity standpoint.

This volume is a necessity in every criminologist's teaching toolbox."

Hillary Potter, *Associate Professor, Department of Ethnic Studies, University of Colorado at Boulder, USA*

TEACHING CRIMINOLOGY AT THE INTERSECTION

A how-to guide for teaching about gender, race, class and sexuality

Edited by
Rebecca M. Hayes, Kate Luther and
Susan Caringella

Routledge
Taylor & Francis Group

LONDON AND NEW YORK

First published 2015
by Routledge
2 Park Square, Milton Park, Abingdon, Oxon, OX14 4RN

and by Routledge
711 Third Avenue, New York, NY 10017

*Routledge is an imprint of the Taylor & Francis Group, an informa
business*

British Library Cataloguing in Publication Data
A catalogue record for this book is available from the British Library

Library of Congress Cataloging-in-Publication Data
Teaching criminology at the intersection : a how-to guide for
teaching about gender, race, class and sexuality / edited by
Rebecca M. Hayes, Kate Luther, Susan Caringella.
pages cm
ISBN 978-0-415-85637-9 (hardback) -- ISBN 978-0-415-85638-6
(paperback) -- ISBN 978-0-203-72614-3 (ebook)
1. Criminology--Study and teaching (Higher) 2. Criminal justice,
Administration of--Study and teaching (Higher) 3. Crime--Sex
differences. 4. Crime and race. 5. Social classes. 6. Discrimination in
criminal justice administration. 7. Criminal behavior--Social aspects.
I. Hayes, Rebecca M. II. Luther, Kate. III. Caringella, Susan.
HV6024.T43 2014
364.071'1--dc23
2014002662

ISBN: 978-0-415-85637-9 (hbk)
ISBN: 978-0-415-85638-6 (pbk)
ISBN: 978-0-203-72614-3 (ebk)

Typeset in Sabon
by Taylor & Francis Books

Printed and bound in Great Britain by
TJ International Ltd, Padstow, Cornwall

CONTENTS

ACKNOWLEDGMENTS

The editors would first like to acknowledge the authors for their amazing contributions. We would also like to give a special thanks to Dr. Joanna Gregson for her insightful comments on the introduction. Additionally, thank you to our research assistants, Jamie Sheppard and Chelsea Monroe, for their assistance on the project. We are also indebted to Brian McNaught for graciously allowing us to reproduce his guided imagery in this book. And, last but not least, a warm thank you to the Division on Women and Crime for inspiring the discussion that led to this book.

NOTES ON CONTRIBUTORS

Elizabeth A. Bradshaw is an Assistant Professor of Sociology at Central Michigan University who specializes in the area of social and criminal justice, specifically the intersection of state and corporate criminality. Her dissertation examined the causes of the Deepwater Horizon explosion and the ensuing response to the 2010 Gulf of Mexico oil spill as a form of state-corporate environmental crime. She is now building on this work to develop the concept of "criminogenic industry structures," and is using this framework to study the hydraulic fracturing industry in Michigan. Beyond state-corporate crime, additional areas of teaching and research include environmental criminology, surveillance, and social movements against corporate globalization.

Kathryn A. Branch is an Assistant Professor in the Department of Criminology and Criminal Justice at the University of Tampa. Her research interests include the impact of sexual assault on secondary victims such as faculty and friends of survivors and the role of social support in women's use of aggression against an intimate partner. Her teaching experience is in Victimology and Family Violence. Her most recent empirical work has been published in *Feminist Criminology*. Along with her co-authors, Dr. Branch was invited to write an article on college student to faculty disclosure of sexual assault and IPV for a special edition of *ELiSS* focused on teaching sensitive topics.

Susan Caringella is an internationally known expert on rape, feminism and criminology. She has published extensively in academic books and journals on topics ranging from rape to violence against women, legislative change, sociological theory, political ideology and public opinion. Her acclaimed book *Addressing Rape Reform in Law and Practice* (2009, Columbia University Press) has been nominated for awards in the American Society of Criminology and the Society for the Study of Social Problems. Professor Caringella's body of scholarship has been widely cited and recognized with national, state, and university scholarship awards and honors.

Walter S. DeKeseredy is Anna Deane Carlson Endowed Chair of Social Sciences and Professor of Sociology at West Virginia University. He has published 18 books and over 160 scientific journal articles and book chapters on violence against women and other social problems. In 2008, the Institute on Violence, Abuse and Trauma gave him the Linda Saltzman Memorial Intimate Partner Violence Researcher Award. He also jointly received the 2004 Distinguished Scholar Award from the American Society of Criminology's (ASC) Division on Women and Crime and the 2007 inaugural University of Ontario Institute of Technology Research Excellence Award. In 1995, he received the Critical Criminologist of the Year Award from the ASC's Division on Critical Criminology (DCC) and in 2008 the DCC gave him the Lifetime Achievement Award.

Rebecca M. Hayes is an Associate Professor in the Department of Sociology, Anthropology and Social Work at Central Michigan University. Driven by her passion for social justice, particularly eradicating violence against women, she assisted with starting the first rape recovery non-profit organization in St. Lucia called PROSAF – Surviving Sexual Abuse in the Caribbean. You can find her scholarly work published in academic journals such as *Feminist Criminology*, *Violence Against Women*, *Crime & Delinquency*, and *Critical Criminology*. In 2013 she was awarded the Central Michigan Vice Provost Award, the American Society of

Criminology's Division on Women and Crime New Scholar Award, and the American Society of Criminology's Division of Victimology Practitioner/Activist of the Year Award.

Paul Hernandez is a former Associate Professor at Central Michigan University and is currently the Director of the High School Turn Around Initiative with the United Way for South East Michigan focusing on improving some of the lowest performing high schools in the country. Before he earned a Ph.D. in Sociology, before his Bachelor's Degree from a university, before his Associate Degree from a community college, Dr. Hernandez was an "at-risk" K-12 student – at risk of dropping out. Today he works with high schools, community colleges and universities to implement a unique pedagogical approach of his own design that helps engage, build meaningful relationships, and improve passing rates with students at risk of dropping out. Dr. Hernandez's research focuses on the sociology of education and social inequality. A hands-on academic, he encourages educators around the country to correspond with him at hernandez.realtalk@gmail.com.

Helen Jones is the Discipline Lead for Sociology and Criminology at The Higher Education Academy. She has taught criminology for almost 20 years at a number of UK universities and also on a US postgraduate course via distance learning. Helen has led a range of teaching and learning initiatives, including the innovative "Murder@" project which delivers a range of virtual authentic projects to universities in the UK and the US. She is a member of the British Sociological Association and executive member of the British Society of Criminology where she leads the Learning and Teaching Network. Helen is also a member of the American Society of Criminology and the Academy of Criminal Justice Sciences. Her research interests span higher education policy, practice and pedagogy, and she has been published on these topics and on issues of gendered violence.

Emily Lenning is an Associate Professor of Criminal Justice at Fayetteville State University. Her publications cover a diverse range of topics, from state-sanctioned violence against women to creative advances in pedagogy. Dr. Lenning has provided Safezone Training to hundreds of faculty, staff and students on her campus in order to foster a safe and inclusive environment for Lesbian, Gay, Bisexual and Transgender (LGBT) students. She is also the co-founder and a representative of her school's Safezone Office, a resource for LGBT students, making Fayetteville State University the third Historically Black University in the entire country to dedicate a Center or Office to issues concerning LGBT students. Dr. Lenning's efforts in and out of the classroom have been recognized by several awards, including the North Carolina Criminal Justice Association's Margaret Lang Willis Outstanding Criminal Justice Educator Award and the American Society of Criminology Division on Women and Crime's New Scholar Award.

Kate Luther is an Assistant Professor of Sociology at Pacific Lutheran University. Her areas of interest include gendered violence, women's incarceration and the impact of incarceration on families. Dr. Luther's current research examines the pathways to college for children of incarcerated parents. She serves as the co-chair for the Division on Women and Crime's Committee for Teaching and Pedagogy.

Tara N. Richards is an Assistant Professor in the School of Criminal Justice at the University of Baltimore. Her major research interests include violence against women; mental health, substance abuse, and trauma/violence; and evaluation research. Her most recent empirical work has been published in *Crime & Delinquency, Violence Against Women,* and *Violence and Victims,* and she is the co-editor of *Sexual Victimization: Then and Now.* Along with her co-authors, Dr. Richards has published research on college student to faculty disclosure of sexual assault and IPV for a special edition of *ELiSS* focused on teaching sensitive topics. She has also been honored by the University of South Florida's Department of Criminology with an Outstanding Criminology Ambassador Alumni Award for her policy relevant scholarship concerning intimate partner violence and her service to adolescent dating violence prevention efforts in the Tampa Bay, Florida area.

Helen Taylor Greene is a Professor in the Department of Administration of Justice in the Barbara Jordan–Mickey Leland School of Public Affairs at Texas Southern University. She is the author, co-author and co-editor with Dr. Shaun L. Gabbidon of several articles, book chapters and books including *Race and Crime*, 3rd ed. (2013, Sage) and *Race and Crime: A Text Reader* (2011, Sage). She also served as lead co-editor of the *Encyclopedia of Race and Crime* (2009, Sage) with Dr. Gabbidon. Dr. Taylor Greene is the recipient of several awards including the 2014 W. E. B. Du Bois Award from the Western Society of Criminology, and the Academy of Criminal Justice Science's Outstanding Mentor Award in 2011.

Toby A. Ten Eyck is an Associate Professor in the Department of Sociology at Michigan State University Extension and Michigan State University. His current research focuses on the intersections of art and social issues, ranging from debates over commissioned statues to the spread of graffiti. He has also studied public opinion and media coverage of food risks.

INTRODUCTION

Rebecca M. Hayes and Kate Luther

As sociologists specializing in inequality in the criminal justice system, we often find ourselves swapping stories with like-minded peers about how difficult it can be to teach about gender, race, class and sexuality, particularly in criminology classes. Students come to our classrooms with their preconceived notions about criminal justice and many expect to learn about policing, incarceration and theories of crimes. Some tend to want to laud the justice system for what they see as an effective and efficient system, and at times seem uninterested in learning about the problems, especially those steeped in inequality. For that reason, professors may face resistance when they ask students to examine how gender impacts victimization, how race affects interactions with the police, how socioeconomic status shapes experiences in court or how sexuality influences treatment in the criminal justice system. Each of these topics – gender, race, class and sexuality – is difficult on its own, and as educators we have the added responsibility of making sure that we explain how social locations also intersect (see Potter, 2014 for a discussion of intersectionality in criminology). This intersection adds complexity, but allows for a more nuanced understanding of privilege and disadvantage.

In order to challenge students to think outside of the box, we must question their preconceived notions of justice in a non-judgmental fashion. Some students come to our courses with strongly held ideas of why women "ask" to be raped or why police officers use racial profiling to catch the "bad guys." As educators, our job is to ask students to recognize and confront their ideologies and as Bransford, Brown and Cocking (2000, p.11) explain:

> There is a good deal of evidence that learning is enhanced when teachers pay attention to the knowledge and beliefs that learners bring to a learning task, use this knowledge as a starting point for new instruction, and monitor students' changing conceptions as instruction proceeds.

Thus, we must understand the worldviews of our students regarding gender, race, class and sexuality as we teach them about criminology and criminal justice.

Throughout this book, the authors illustrate a critical pedagogical approach. Following Paulo Freire's *Pedagogy of the oppressed* (1970), the authors argue for creating a dialogue between professors and their students when teaching sensitive topics. Instead of following the "banking" model of education, where professors primarily "deposit" information in students, the authors focus on the conversation between students and teachers as they mutually engage the material. Furthermore, these authors clearly support opportunities for students to take what they have learned in the classroom and use it in the "real" world. As Fobes and Kaufman (2008, p.27) so poignantly described it, "the distinguishing feature of critical pedagogy is that it is both a form of practice and a form of action … it also implores us to use our teaching and learning to effect positive social change." This is especially significant in the field of criminology as many of our students plan to work in policing, courts, corrections and victim services – areas that are ripe with potential for enacting social change.

As educators, we want to best prepare our students to be sensitive to issues of gender, race, social class and sexuality in their future careers and lives. At the same time, many of us struggle with how exactly to teach this material. We learned to think critically about these topics in our graduate training; however, many academics never received training on *how* to become effective teachers. The reality of academe is that the majority of outgoing Ph.D.s will land jobs at universities where there will be a focus on their competency in the classroom. Especially for those new assistant professors who must demonstrate teaching excellence for tenure and promotion, this book provides a "how-to" guide for teaching some of the most contentious topics in criminology.

In order to frame this book, we begin by sharing about ourselves as teachers, describing the challenges we face in the classroom and the approaches we use when teaching about gender, race, class and sexuality. We note that our stories are anecdotal and, as such, are shaped by our social location (e.g., gender, race, class, sexuality, etc.), but also the context of our universities. Both university context and student population make a difference for classroom climate and the ability to create a safe space. University context, such as the location of the university, whether it is public or private, if it is religiously affiliated and the overall institutional climate, will influence teaching practices. Additionally, student population makeup including race, ethnicity, class and sexuality will affect student reactions to the material, even if only subtly. It is our hope that we have provided a breadth of experience in this volume that addresses many different contexts and environments, but before trying any specific tactic, we think it is important to be mindful of your university context.

Rebecca's approach

In the classroom, my overarching goal is to have students question their assumptions about our social world, particularly regarding how the criminal justice system operates. I want to challenge students not to see the offender as the "bad guy" or "the other," but to empathize or at least attempt to understand where they may be coming from. "Othering" occurs when "a dominant group defines into existence an inferior group" and includes "the invention of categories and ideas about what marks people as belonging to these categories" (Schwalbe, et al., 2000, p.422). The notion of offenders as "crazy" is one of the most prevalent examples of "othering" in my classes and this is hopefully laid to rest when we focus on the social circumstances that often lead individuals down a path to crime and deviant behavior. I attempt to explain that "othering" often serves as a distancing tool whereby one places themselves in a superior position to the individual that is "othered." A useful way I have found to decrease "othering" is the use of a self-report survey called, "Everyone's a Criminal."

In my Introduction to Social and Criminal Justice class, we start with an activity where students admit to their own criminal behavior, which begins the deconstruction of the criminal as "the other" (see Reichel, 1982). Originally suggested by Reichel, students respond to a checklist of about 20 items that are deviant and illegal behavior, by marking a check by the number on a blank piece of paper. Then I reveal the punishment for each crime. At the end they total the amount of fines and jail time. Finally by a show of hands I ask how many folks have to go to jail, which in my ten years of teaching I have only had one class where a person did not raise their hand. The epiphany occurs when they look around and see that everyone has committed some type of behavior where they could have ended up in the criminal justice system. This not only dismantles the "othering," but it also assists with creating a classroom environment where we recognize that we are all human and therefore have many similarities.

Recognizing the humanity in each other is part of my teaching approach which is concerned with building rapport and a sense of community in the classroom. When students are comfortable in the classroom, they will be more open and honest about their preconceived notions regarding the criminal justice system. If they remain silent, I will be unable to assist in the examination and deconstruction of their current ideologies. In all my classes, I invite students on the first day to ask me all sorts of questions with the understanding that if I feel it is too personal, I reserve the right to not answer. It is mentioned over and over again the importance of respecting each other in the classroom, but at the same time I emphasize that I want them to be open and honest about their opinions. By creating this classroom environment, it is easier for us to delve into more complicated topics of stereotypes, privilege and advantage in the context of the criminal justice system.

Kate's approach

My goal each semester is to encourage students to understand the particular topic of study, whether juvenile delinquency, corrections, gendered violence or criminological theory, through the lens of the sociological imagination (Mills, 1959). Mills argued that we commonly understand social problems as personal "troubles" rather than public "issues." Following Mills' sociological imagination, I work to create a classroom environment where students can understand the social forces that influence criminal offending and subsequent interactions with the criminal justice system.

In creating this type of learning environment, I have also learned that the challenges we face in the classroom vary by university and that we need to be aware of the makeup of the student population. As a graduate student, I had vastly different experiences teaching Sociology of Corrections at two universities. At the large racially diverse public university, there was no need to convince students of the inequalities in the criminal justice system. Many students had direct or indirect experience with the correctional system and the knowledge they were gaining in the classroom only confirmed what they already knew. In contrast, teaching the same course at the small conservative Christian university was completely different because of the students' backgrounds and level of privilege. Thinking about inequality was a relatively new experience for many of them and thus I had to significantly adjust my approach to teaching about the correctional system. Although I no longer teach at either of these universities, I learned how student demographics shape responses to course material.

This last point brings up the issue of variability among students in a classroom. Even though the majority of students may fit within a particular demographic, we must recognize that there is always a portion of students who come from different backgrounds than the majority. For example, when teaching about the fear of crime, I focus discussion around the fear that some students have when they venture off of campus to enter the surrounding community. Although some students express a degree of apprehension of the outside area, there are students who grew up in the community or feel very safe leaving campus. I highlight this variability in fear of crime and allow students to give voice to experiences that vary greatly from the majority of their classmates. As educators, it is important for us to not marginalize the perspectives of students who are not part of the majority at our particular institution.

Overview of the book

Although we teach criminology at different universities (a public state university versus a private liberal arts university), in vastly different areas of the country (Midwest versus the Pacific Northwest), we find that we struggle with similar issues in the classroom – teaching our students to recognize their privilege/oppression, overcoming stereotypes and moving away from framing criminal offenders as "the other." Of course, the way in which we experience those challenges are different, but based on our understanding of these common challenges in the criminology and criminal justice classroom, we have brought together a group of excellent college professors to contribute to this text. We invited them to discuss how they teach topics ranging from race and crime to women as both offenders and victims. Each contributor discusses how they teach a contemporary criminal justice issue, while grounding their approach in the academic literature. Additionally, our contributors have included examples of activities, assignments and resources they have successfully used to teach these complicated topics.

Paul Hernandez and Toby Ten Eyck begin the book with their lesson on "The social construction of a monster." This activity is sociologically informed and uses the concepts of schema, prototypical thinking and terministic screen, which helps us teach our students how society has constructed the idea of who is a "monster." Chapter 1 sets the stage to discuss race in a less defensive manner that should result in lower levels of student resistance. The beauty of this approach is its applicability to much of what we teach in criminology and criminal justice, whether it be the social construction of criminals, victims or crime.

However, if students get defensive or become sensitive to the material, Chapter 2 by Kathryn Branch and Tara Richards covers how to handle these delicate student situations. In "Research on teaching sensitive topics: a review of the challenges and opportunities for enhancing the classroom experience," Branch and Richards discuss how to approach each situation with a non-judgmental manner and level of empathy that will both connect the students with the material and not negate their personal experiences.

Victim blaming, especially for gender-related victimization, occurs all too frequently and the next author navigates this deconstruction of knowledge with ease. Helen Jones takes us inside her approach to teaching victimology. Chapter 3, "Self-reflection in motion: the victimology classroom," covers student disclosures of both offending and victimization and presents the reader with suggestions for teaching about this complicated topic.

To further the discussion on sensitive topics, Helen Taylor Greene invites us to step into her classroom and learn how she teaches about race and ethnicity in the context of crime. In Chapter 4, "Still at the periphery: teaching race, ethnicity, crime, and justice," Taylor Greene carefully addresses the historical context of studying race in criminology, the challenges facing faculty who teach this topic and best practices to minimize student resistance in the classroom.

In Chapter 5, "The invisible minority: making the LGBT community visible in the criminal justice classroom," Emily Lenning shows how both society and criminal justice education ignores LGBT victimizations and the criminalization of sexuality. She makes a compelling argument for why we need to train our future criminal justice workers to be sensitive to issues of sexuality. Lenning's argument is coupled with a thought-provoking activity that encourages students to think about their sexuality and how it impacts their day-to-day experiences.

Next, Chapter 6 addresses how to broaden students' perspectives on who commits crime and how we define crime. Elizabeth Bradshaw shares her expertise on how to teach students to look beyond their socially constructed ideas of crime as "street crime." Her chapter, "Filling the void: classroom strategies for teaching about crimes of the powerful," focuses on teaching about white collar, corporate and state crime, with attention to the role of the media and mainstream criminology in perpetuating the idea of what is and is not thought of as criminal.

Walter DeKeseredy rounds out the book in Chapter 7, "Women are more than victims: gender, crime and the criminal justice system." He carefully explains the complexity of teaching about gender and crime, while taking into account the socio-political context. In particular, DeKeseredy points out how often the criminal justice curriculum (and society) paints women as victims and does not take notice of the other roles women play in the criminal justice system.

To our knowledge, there is not one tried and true way to effectively teach about inequality. Instead, it is helpful to have a toolkit full of different examples, activities and approaches. We hope that through this book, the many different approaches to teaching inequality we provide will give you a new toolset to use in your own classroom – or, at the very least, remind you that you are not alone in your struggles.

Bibliography

Bransford, J.D., Brown, A.L. and Cocking, R.R. eds., 2000. *How people learn: Brain, mind, experience, and school – Expanded edition*. Washington, DC: National Academy Press.

Fobes, C. and Kaufman, P., 2008. Critical pedagogy in the sociology classroom: Challenges and concerns. *Teaching Sociology*, 36, pp.26–33.

Freire, P., 1970. *Pedagogy of the oppressed*. New York: Herder and Herder.

Mills, C.W., 1959. *The sociological imagination*. New York: Oxford University Press.

Potter, H., 2014. *Intersectionality and criminology: Gender, race, class and crime*. London: Routledge.

Reichel, P.L., 1982. A criminal activities checklist. *Teaching Sociology*, 10, pp.94–97.

Schwalbe, M., Godwin, S., Holden, D., Schrock, D., Thompson, S. and Wolkomir, M., 2000. Generic processes in the reproduction of inequality: An interactionist analysis. *Social Forces*, 79(2), pp.419–52.

1

THE SOCIAL CONSTRUCTION OF A MONSTER

A lesson from a lecture on race

Paul Hernandez and Toby A. Ten Eyck

Discussing the social construction of race and differences in college classrooms has proven to be difficult (Obach, 1999; Townsley, 2007; Khanna and Harris, 2009). Race is especially challenging to teach in classrooms that have little diversity and/or where the instructor is a member of a socially privileged group (Bohmer and Briggs, 1991; Pence and Fields, 1999; Haddad and Lieberman, 2002; Harlow, 2009). When discussing racial inequality and racism and linking these topics to broader society, professors and students are often resistant or uncomfortable, making it difficult to know if the presented material is being processed in a critical manner. Overall, introducing students to material that challenge their preconceived ideas within society is difficult. This is especially true when teaching students to critically examine our socially constructed understanding of criminals. For example, students may have the idea that crime in society is a product of inherently dangerous African American and Latino men, or that poor minority communities are filled with "bad" people who are criminals. Students are inundated by media imagery which shape their perceptions of inequality within the justice system and race-based sentencing (Alexander, 2010), immigration (Zatz, 2012), women, drugs and prison (Bush-Baskette, 2010) or racial profiling (Gabbidon, et al., 2012). A common thread among many of the common topics illuminated by the media is race. Race seems to be a central topic among the majority, if not all topics engaged by the criminal system in the United States. Thus, when examining the many issues presented in criminal justice courses, it is critical to confront racial bias or discomfort or any "untouchable" topics surrounding race and difference. Many students are convinced that they can determine people's race based on visual observation and phenotype or that along with race are undeniable predetermined qualities based on stereotypes. Students come to our classrooms with their socialization from parents, peers, media and society. With a lifetime of believing that the majority of their ideas are social facts, combined with entering a course that challenges these ideas, the stage is set for resistance from students when teaching about the social construction of criminals.

Privilege also plays a role in the development of many of the ideas that students bring to class. Students' privileges can work as something that makes them exempt to negative stereotypes which they often accuse other groups of possessing. If the instructor responds with frustration to seemingly off-target questions or student apathy, she or he can potentially shut down the students' willingness to participate; thus creating an environment where students are unlikely to be open to sociological perspectives on race.

This chapter offers an interactive lecture on the social construction of race influenced by Dr. Ten Eyck but created and implemented by Dr. Hernandez. I have used this material, titled "The Social Construction of a Monster," in introductory to sociology, race and inequality, contemporary social problems, and social inequality courses in both a major university and community college. The class sizes at both institutions were similar with approximately 35–40 students. The majority of students were non-sociology majors fulfilling core academic requirements and were European American from small rural communities that likely had little, if any, racial diversity.

The underlying motivation for this work is similar to that of Bohmer and Briggs (1991), in that my attempts in the classroom to explore complex racial topics with students from privileged class and race backgrounds have often been met with antagonistic, confused or indifferent reactions. I have found that it is often difficult for students to understand race relations beyond their own individual, anecdotal explanations and experiences (or lack thereof), and are likely to draw on the myths and stereotypes of race presented by the media and treat these as part of their known realities. For example, many of my students typically believe that issues surrounding race are historical and today those who claim racism are simply "playing the race card." When students share that they have never personally experienced racism or that they are not racist, they further emphasize that they do not understand how racism is problematic. Lastly, some of my students have shared that racism is something that only happens in very isolated areas with uneducated individuals. They see racism apart from themselves as "people different than them" because they themselves do not see the "color" of people. When these views are combined with a lack of sociological insight and a lack of understanding of the structure behind racial and social stratification in America, this becomes an obstacle for students' development and learning. This lack of understanding creates a distinct barrier for many students as they fail to develop insight to and knowledge surrounding the reality of racism and social discrimination present in the criminal justice system.

In order to address their resistance, "The Social Construction of a Monster" lecture is effective as it shifts the focus from specific racial groups and moves it to important sociological concepts. This lecture aids in the understanding of race specifically and how the media plays into the social construction of reality, generally. This is accomplished by using concepts recognizable to many readers within sociology, but applying them to an uncommon subject material for most social science courses: the American Pit Bull Terrier (APBT). This strategy helps break students' barriers of discomfort and stimulates them to be open and receptive to concepts surrounding race in America.

Student resistance

The idea of race as a social construction is common in Sociology. Winant (2000, p.172) provides an insightful definition of this concept, "At its most basic level, race can be defined as a concept that signifies and symbolizes sociopolitical conflicts and interests in reference to different types of human bodies ... categories employed to differentiate among ... groups reveal themselves, upon serious examination, to be imprecise if not completely arbitrary."

Due to the socio-political nature of the discussion on race, my in-class experiences have demonstrated that students struggle to accept this idea. They often respond by either tuning out or showing minimal interest in the topic. This has led to trying to find new ways of connecting race to discrimination in contemporary America (Gamson, 1992).

Student resistance to the idea of modern racism is routinely encountered. Modern racism is the idea that prejudice has become a labyrinth of subtle, complex, and negative foundations, where the expression of racial hostilities happens indirectly (Healey, 2010). Many students struggle with this notion because they focus on racism as an isolated, random problem caused by ill-intentioned people that involve overt behaviors. Students blame "old people" or extremists for racism in society (Harlow, 2009), rarely viewing themselves as displaying potentially discriminatory behaviors.

When race is brought up in sociology or criminology classrooms, often European American students contend that racism is not a problem. These students struggle to view themselves as people of privilege regarding race and often talk about race in terms of minorities receiving special treatment due to affirmative action. They use examples such as their parents losing jobs or that they will be limited in their local job prospects after graduation due to affirmative action. These stereotypes make it difficult for them to see how groups are disadvantaged. Haddad and Lieberman (2002, p.331) stated "once white students recognize their advantages, they have to acknowledge that institutionalized inequality not only exists but favors them." It is difficult for students to come to the realization of their own systemic privilege and shift away from viewing society as individualistic where one's conditions are largely the product of their own choosing (Obach, 2000). Concepts developed by researchers of mass media and race can be used to facilitate these changes. That is, through a demonstration of how the media influences public opinion students are able to see how stereotypes are formed and how these stereotypes become social facts.

The American Pit Bull Terrier

I specifically chose the American Pit Bull Terrier (APBT) for this lecture because of its consistent negative portrayal by the news media for the past thirty years. This portrayal has led to the development of institutionalized discrimination against the breed. The media has been a driving force behind the social construction of the APBT's image, though any coverage on the breed's history and temperament are often lacking. Instead, the reporting reflects the phrase "if it bleeds, it leads" when framing the use of violence in the news (see Entman and Rojecki, 2000). In the 1980s, the U.S. media exploded with stories focusing on the APBT. The breed was tied to dog fighting, drug dealers, and gang members. In the early 1980s, the APBT was already on pace to become the breed known as the super predator (Delise, 2007).

The solidification of the breed as "natural born killers" came in a series of magazine articles published in the late 1980s. On July 6, 1987, *People* magazine published a story titled "An Instinct for the Kill" focusing on the APBT and addressing the ferocity and power of the breed. The APBT was labeled "the Rambo of the dog world" and was reported "to have a biting force of 1800 lbs per square inch" (Green, 1987, p.30). Following suit, *Sports Illustrated* (Swift, 1987) featured a front cover of an APBT in an attacking stance showing snarling teeth with the accompanying words, "Beware of this Dog." The article's focus was on dog fighting in general, though it portrayed the APBT as ferocious and unreliable.

Time, which is recognized as one of the most popular magazines in the United States and is also competitive worldwide (Time Inc., 2013), ran an article on the APBT in the same month as *Sports Illustrated*. The title of the article was "Behavior: Time Bomb on Legs," and began:

> Fire burst from its open mouth, its eyes glowed with a smolder-ing glare, its muzzle and hackles and dewlap were outlined in flickering flame. Never in the delirious dream of a disordered brain could anything more savage, more appalling, more hellish, be conceived than that dark form and savage face. It is as if the vicious hound of the Baskervilles that burst upon Sherlock Holmes out of the fog has returned to haunt the streets of America. The creature last week attacked …
>
> *(Brand, 1987, p.60)*

This portrayal continued through coverage by both print and broadcast media outlets. No longer a dog, the APBT had become a monster. With powerful and consistently negative media coverage, more myths than facts continued to be fed to the public. Throughout the 1990s, the media remained focused on the APBT as an aggressive, dangerous dog. The mass hysteria that was conjured in the 1980s carried through the 1990s and has become a normalized opinion of the APBT (Delise, 2007).

The concerns generated by the media led to the creation of Breed Specific Legislation (BSL) in a number of states. This is "legislation that attempts to deal with the valid concern over vicious dog attacks by irrationally banning or strictly regulating the ownership of pit bulls ... " (Burstein, 2004, p.314). The BSL relayed messages to the public that have plagued the APBT based on irrational and unfounded scientific claims. For example, "some experts even believe that the presence of hormones in children of puberty age can set off Pit bulls" (Delise, 2007, p.113) without identifying a single expert, noting that most dog breeds have the ability to detect hormones, or providing empirical evidence of such statements. More specifically the APBT has been singled out and determined to be like no other breed based on claims of behavior exclusive to the APBT. "Pit bulls inflict more serious wounds than other breeds because they tend to attack the deep muscles, to hold, to shake, and cause ripping of tissue" (p.121). What is not mentioned, however, is that this behavior, tearing, shaking, and holding, is characteristic of most cases of dog bites by many breeds of dogs that have been recorded in official court records (Delise, 2007). Countless claims have been made of actions or characteristics supposedly exclusive to the APBT, though, it is rare to find evidence of such claims or relation to any specific case involving the APBT. Actions taken against the APBT are proof of how pseudoscience and discrimination can lead to laws enacted to confront what people have been told to fear.

This legacy of negative media coverage and established societal norms makes the use of this animal an ideal example to demonstrate sociological concepts surrounding the social construction of our reality. Students can further connect the social constructions of a breed while trying to navigate their own ideas of institutionalized racism. Analyzing these ideas through non-human subject matter, students are able to freely grapple with these concepts and realize the applicability within their own lives, viewpoints, and society. By focusing on dogs, students typically do not feel defensive, worry about who is listening to what they say, or carefully judging exactly what they say in order to remain politically correct and in "good standing" with those around them. The focus on dogs allows them to speak freely and openly without any worries of being judged or critiqued regarding their views. They also move away from their rigid ideas that typically target people or society allowing them to be more willing to learn new things that would typically immediately challenge their ideas.

The interactive lecture

Students in general commonly use the media as a source of understanding the topics discussed in criminal justice classrooms. Given the lack of racial diversity in many students' hometowns, media and the images it portrays is used as a guide when thinking about the many themes within criminal justice, and in this case, specifically race and race relations. The use of three main concepts helps translate media images into this lecture's material: schema, prototypical thinking, and terministic screen, all of which can help students better understand their cultural assumptions about race in America. Combining these three concepts allows students to develop insight into how people view and interpret their social environments. Many students are unaware of their own filters, as well as how these filters have been constructed for them, when making decisions about animals and people. Focusing on the APBT aids in identifying how their views are formed, often with little or no direct experience. By showing them how their attitudes toward the APBT have been created and maintained, we can often make a smoother and more comfortable transition into discussions of race. Basically, before students can fully grasp the racial inequalities in the criminal justice system, they must first address their own socially constructed ideas of race.

In order to transition to discussions of race, I deliver the "The Social Construction of a Monster" lecture with PowerPoint™. To begin I instruct the class to not take notes during the presentation because each person's involvement is important. I engage students by asking questions based on the content associated with each slide. As I ask them questions it helps bring their attention and engagement to the forefront of the lecture helping make them part of the teaching process.

First, I introduce the concept of schema which is defined as "a set of related concepts that allow people to make inferences about new information based on already organized prior knowledge. Schema (is) abstract generic knowledge that holds across many particular instances" (Entman and Rojecki, 2000, p.48). I elaborate that people's schema helps them understand the world around them, making it possible to navigate the social environment without having to (re)negotiate every situation and encounter. While this makes social interactions much more efficient, it can also lead to judgments based on mediated realities. These realities often have been developed from interests in particular power structures that may or may not serve an individual's own interests. Further explanation of this scholarly definition is provided by way of examples such as, "What comes to mind when I describe my buddy Dave as a rich guy?" or "What comes to mind when I say, my buddy is poor?" In three years of using this approach, three consistent categories have emerged regarding the rich guy: material possessions, personality characteristics, and demographic impressions. Common responses are: nice car, big house, snobby, hardworking, educated, and white. Common responses regarding the poor guy include having a "crappy" car, no education, no job, dirty, lazy, and lives in the ghetto. It is imperative to respond positively to any response in order to avoid making students feel judged or attacked.

Whether the student contributes in a positive manner or makes an offensive comment, it is important to utilize their responses as part of the lesson. For example, once during the activity of describing my buddy who is poor, a student loudly spouted out, "a minority." Rather than chastising this student for stereotyping based on race or gender, I further questioned him, asking him for clarification, as an attempt to bring to the forefront that his statement was founded on a stereotype rather than fact. In the case where a student's response is highly offensive or confrontational, I redirect the response using different language or by merely stating, "I wouldn't state it that way, but how else would you describe it?" constantly trying to get at the "why" behind the responses to help expose stereotypes. Whether I agree with their perspectives or not, it is through the lesson that they are guided through a process that challenges their preconceived views. By explaining the unconscious use of schema in their responses by stating that although they do not know my buddy, by using words such as "rich" and "poor" they have already formed their own ideas and images of him.

The second slide defines prototypical thinking where I demonstrate how the media reinforces cultural assumptions. Prototypical thinking occurs when "the most representative members are called prototypical. Prototype theory posits that people abstract out a central tendency – a summary mental representation of a concept – sometimes based on experience but often on ideal characteristics derived from cultural lessons" (Entman and Rojecki, 2000, p.61). Prototypical thinking reinforces schema as it further solidifies personal views of society influenced by media surrounding various issues or topics, such as the APBT. As developed by the media, the term "pit bull" has become representative of what people often envision as an aggressive, violent, and destructive dog.

To facilitate this discussion, I use an example of birds that Entman and Rojenki (2000) discussed in their book *The Black Image in the White Mind: Media and Race in America*. They argue that when people are asked to think of birds, they most commonly answer "robin" or "sparrow" as the prototypical birds. I ask students to, "Tell me what type of bird comes to mind when I say the word 'bird.'" Similar to Entman and Rojenki, common answers were "robin," "sparrow," "blue jay," and "cardinal" (common Midwestern species), showing regional impact on prototypical thinking. Positive reinforcement is given after which I explain how they have used prototypical thinking to a common, though general word.

I remind students that although the birds mentioned are birds, there is not one bird more representative of the bird family than any other. In other words, there is nothing inherent about a blue jay that makes it more "bird-like" than an ostrich or penguin. We discuss the world's range of bird species but note that with 30–40 individuals in the room only a few specific birds were identified. Students realize their use of prototypical thinking in displaying similar associations of "bird" as the most representative of "bird" in their culture. I reiterate the notion of schema and how it is used in combination with prototypical thinking to formulate perspectives in how people view the world.

The last concept, terministic screen, is introduced as "vocabularies ... particular to members of socioeconomic, cultural, professional, or other kinds of groups. Within these vocabularies, group members understand aspects of 'reality' in different ways because each terministic vocabulary encourages members to 'select' portions of 'reality' while 'deflecting' others" (Rockler, 2002, p.400). I elaborate on this definition with examples that help connect terministic screen to everyday thoughts and ideas that help people to interpret what they see. Common examples of gender and social class are used to help students understand these connections and to help them identify their own constructed views of both dogs and people. I explain how gender affects people's view of the world through different experiences between men and women. One example is the image of a man leaving his place of employment late at night with no one around as he has to walk a few blocks to get to his car. As a man and through my terministic screen, when walking to my car I am aware of my surroundings but the last thing on my mind, or actually something I do not even think about, is the potential of being raped or sexually assaulted. My terministic screen is not focused on the culture of rape, but this does not mean that it does not exist or that it is not a disturbing problem within society. In contrast, for many women the same scenario brings forth through their terministic screen the awareness of the potential for rape or sexual assault.

Next, I explain how a personal wager of five, one hundred, or one thousand dollars can be perceived quite differently to people of varying socioeconomic classes. For example, as a university professor my social class is typically much higher than my students thus through my terministic screen a bet of one hundred dollars would likely be on par with a 20 dollar bet for a college student. Through a student's terministic screen, one hundred dollars is more likely to be viewed as a significant risk. We further discuss how our perceptions and understanding of the world are influenced by our race, class, gender, sexuality, and education.

The fourth slide demonstrates how schema, prototypical thinking, and terministic screen are used in everyday life. This slide is titled "News Headlines." First, I ask the class to tell me what breed of dog comes to mind after reading each headline. The first states, "Dog Saves Young Boy from Fire." The class calls out responses all of which I attempt to acknowledge to encourage involvement and excitement. As answers slow, I repeat some of the breeds: Dalmatians, Golden Retrievers, and Collies. The actual breed of dog that saved the boy by waking him up during the fire was a Jack Russell Terrier.

The second headline states "Dog Attacks 2nd Child in 4 Years." The majority of students I have encountered respond with "pit bull." Other breeds such as the Rottweiler and Doberman Pincher are also mentioned but are not as commonly shared, nor as enthusiastically. Many are surprised when I reveal that the story is about an American Bull Dog. Once students have reflected on the answer, I return to the APBT and ask students to share information or facts they know about this breed. Once students provide their ideas and opinions, I move to discuss APBT myths and facts.

The fifth slide is titled "Myth vs. Fact" and focuses on media generated stories surrounding the APBT. The left side of the slide focuses on the myths of the breed including the colloquial tale of the "lock jaw, the breed's 1800 pounds per square inch (psi) bite force,"[1] and its mean and vicious nature. After going over this information, I reveal the facts on the right side of the slide.

The first fact is that there is "no scientific evidence of a 'locking mechanism'." Dog experts Drs. Howard Evans, Sandy DeLahunta, and Katherine Houpt state, "we all agree that the power [in the APBT] bite is proportional to the size of the jaws and the jaw muscles. There is no anatomical structure that could be a locking mechanism" (Delise, 2007, p.109). The APBT's powerful bite force is another popular myth and adds to its aura of violence. I explain that a bite force of 1800 psi is closer to that of a crocodile than any domestic dog in existence. To combat this myth, I use a YouTube clip of a National Geographic animal bite study during the lecture to illustrate tests and results of bite force titled "Bite Force Competition … " (National Geographic, 2009). This clip debunks the myth of the APBT's bite force impressing upon students the plethora of myths they have often come to accept as fact.

The final myth is the APBT's natural, irrevocably mean and vicious temperament. I use results from the national non-profit American Temperament Test Society (2013) to challenge this myth and show what the test measures across all dog breeds. The definition of canine temperament is "the sum total of all inborn and acquired physical and mental traits and talents which determines forms and regulates behavior in the environment." Recent average passing rates for the APBT is 86.8 percent versus 83 percent for all other breeds demonstrating that the APBT passes the sound temperament test at higher rates than other breeds such as Collies (80.3 percent), Golden Retriever (85.2 percent) and Dalmatian (82.7 percent). The American Temperament Test Society's Operations Director has asserted that, "I have personally tested … these dogs and have found them to be nice, polite, and non-aggressive, even the dogs that failed our test. Failures occurred not for aggression, but for strong avoidance to one or more of the subtests" (Comstock, 2009). Data collected for over thirty years helps to discredit the breeds' inherently mean and vicious myth.

Finishing the Myth vs. Fact slide, I reiterate the three concepts of schema, prototypical thinking, and terministic screen. We discuss how these concepts have turned myth into fact concerning the APBT. I make a point of showing how uncritical thinking on their part has led to an understanding of the world that does not mesh with scientific facts. Next, is a game where they will get another chance to see how these concepts are used.

The sixth and seventh slides are the "game" aspect of the lecture which I refer to as, "Find the APBT." Slide 6 has 15 numbered pictures of different breeds of dogs including the American Bully and Cane Corso, both of which are commonly mistaken as the APBT. The class has two minutes to choose the dog they think is the APBT, and they are told they can move around the room if they need a closer or different viewpoint. When the time is up they verbally share their answers, as well as how they came to that conclusion. They usually share the logic behind their decisions based on seeing an APBT in person, in the media, or via descriptions from friends or family. I then ask the class if they would like to see the names of all the breeds on the next slide, which always yields a unanimous yes. Such a response is proof that there is at least some level of engagement within the class.

The seventh slide lists the breed names with each dog's picture and number, and it is at this point that students realize that most have gotten the APBT wrong (on average approximately less than 10 percent of my students can correctly identity an APBT out of this lineup). First, I point out the APBT and explain the aesthetic and behavioral standards of this breed according to United Kennel Club and American

Dog Breeders Association. Then we discuss the other dogs, providing their distinct backgrounds, and explain how they are commonly mistaken for the APBT. Then, I extend a brief summary of the prevalent media depiction of the APBT and explain the impact that schema, prototypical thinking, and terministic screen have on their perceptions. We discuss how these perceptions have an impact on turning myths into facts, which in turn will influence how they negotiate certain parts of the social – and natural – landscape.

The lecture is ended by sharing facts regarding current laws and policies against the breed resulting from misconceptions held by the media, public, and lawmakers. Discrimination that exists against the APBT is overt which makes it easier for students to distinguish how the social construction of "breed" (race) contributes to "discrimination" (racism). Students are able to openly discuss this phenomenon through the non-threatening example of a breed of dog, and it is at this point the lecture is transitioned into a discussion of race.

The final slide is titled "News Headlines" which lists the following four headlines: "Man Accused in Love Triangle Murder," "Gang-Members Brawl in Open Court," "Illegal Immigrants Taking Jobs from Americans," and "Terrorists Attack Hotel with Tourists." These headlines were chosen in an online search of news articles, and students are made aware that these are headlines that appeared in print. Each headline is presented separately so that students are asked what type of person comes to mind when they read the words. Responses are often connected to race. This demonstrates how students unconsciously use schema, prototypical thinking, and terministic screening on a daily basis when thinking about different groups of people. More specifically, these concepts shape ideas of different racial groups with which they have likely had little experiential contact.

Modern racism is introduced at this point, and I explain that while legal barriers have been abolished, contemporary ideas about racial groups, highlighted with dog breeds, provide a framework for thinking about particular racial groups. We then discuss how this framework permeates our dominant institutions such as the criminal justice, educational, and business systems. It is expected that students will begin to make the connections between discrimination against a constructed monster, the APBT, and attitudes toward racial groups. It is at this point that the sociological imagination begins to click as students come to an understanding regarding the importance of being critical consumers of mass media. Students begin to share that they had no idea that their social facts were grounded on myths and they begin to think beyond the routines of daily life. Students begin to question their own ideas and sources as they begin to see things beyond the limitations they had set for themselves.

Student responses

In order to assess the effectiveness of the lecture, student evaluations were conducted. Students were invited to answer two evaluative questions, both of which were voluntary and anonymous. The questions were "Did you like or dislike the lecture? Please explain why." and "Did you learn anything from this lesson? Please explain." After explaining the instructions, I leave the room to avoid influence on the responses and a student collects the responses and brings them to my office.

Out of four classes ($N = 108$) that provided feedback 96 percent answered they "liked" the lecture, with 3 percent answering that they did not like the lecture, and 1 percent not answering the question. The open-ended responses were coded into three themes: student interaction, critical development, and personal connection. The theme of student interaction focuses around the student's identification of engagement and interaction with the lesson, professor, and peers. An example of student interaction was provided by one student's reply:

> I really enjoyed this lesson because it wasn't just a professor throwing facts at the class and then having to write them down. I usually get sleepy during those types of lectures. I liked how this was interactive and it really made me think more than that other type of lecture.

The student explained a level of interest and involvement that they usually find missing in standard lecture formats. Another student stated, "I can understand how asking about race can make people uncomfortable. By using dogs you were able to show how we automatically come up with ideas about certain breeds without making people feel uncomfortable about what they thought. You were able to get us talking about what normally is uncomfortable by making it comfortable." The student perceived my latent intent of the lecture: by focusing on dogs we can get past the uncomfortable and difficult task of presenting race with little or no introduction.

Another theme is critical development which focuses on students learning something related to content or being able to critically assess or evaluate what they learn in regards to larger, sociological concepts. Of the respondents, 82 percent revealed learning something in relation to stereotypes (18 percent stated prior familiarity with the dog examples). A typical example from this was, "I definitely learned more because it was so interesting. Asking us to say what we thought of with the specific [news headlines] really made me realize how we all attach stereotypes to specific races and social classes." This student alludes to how he/she learned to connect the formation of racial stereotypes to larger, structural factors such as the media. Another student wrote, "I enjoyed this lesson very much. I thought that using dogs as an example of our own stereotypes was an appropriate way to make the connection to our other, larger stereotypes." Another student discussed mental images regarding the news headlines, "I was a little surprised how quickly stereotypes jumped to mind, even when intellectually I know most of them are not accurate. It seems in the modern American schema that terrorists either wear turbans or dress like the Unabomber." Overall, the students described learning how stereotypes and discrimination against racial groups are systemically propagated and how these ideas and images are powerfully embedded into an individual's thinking.

The final set of responses encompassed a theme of personal connection. These students not only shared their enthusiasm for the lesson but mentioned personal feelings, some referencing their families. One student explained:

> I own a lab/pit mix, and it is the friendliest dog that I know, yet when I hear about pit bulls, I still think of them as vicious creatures. The awareness that I do the same thing with people is startling. I feel ashamed that I have these stereotypes ingrained in my mind. I know some of the facts and yet I choose to ignore them. It is discouraging. I hope that from now on, I will use

reason and logic to deduce my thoughts instead of jumping to the stereotype embedded in my mind.

This student's insights show the lesson's ability to connect the influences of personal views to social issues. Such a connection was made by another student:

I liked the activity about naming the bird that first came to our mind because it reminded me of how the media uses races. For example African American males are criminals or football players. Asian Americans are smart and good in math. I should show this PowerPoint to my parents.

That the student had a desire to relate this to parents points to another agent in the socialization process, and one that would be interesting to incorporate in later versions of this lecture. The final comment truly represents the overall goal of my efforts "I didn't think I was a very judgmental person but to all the headlines, I had a very distinct picture in my head. I learned I shouldn't make assumptions or pass this along to family members and friends." This speaks of the lecture's ability to impact students' perspectives on race relations.

Conclusion

The social construction of a monster lecture introduces the politically charged topic of race in a non-threatening manner which promotes a comfortable atmosphere. Rather than provoking the initial defensiveness or filtered comments we often see when discussing race, it fosters receptiveness to concepts through the use of subject material on the APBT. Students begin to understand how they discriminate against people without offering facts or facing them personally. This presentation is not forceful or blameful of who is, or seems to be, racist in society. Rather, it helps students understand their potential of having negative views of racial groups in a society that has been promoted by the media and others.

This lecture is not one that is bound to race alone. It is extremely flexible and can be used effectively to teach about many socially constructed concepts addressed in criminology courses. For example, students have socially constructed ideas of who is a criminal and what constitutes a crime. The only change would come in the final slide of the lecture which can be adjusted to whichever topic the presenter sees fit. Changing the last slide to represent images students have in mind by using different news headlines representing different types of crimes (e.g. "Woman robbed at gunpoint in downtown," "Drug Dealers increasing violence across the country," etc. ...). The lecture is ultimately able to address a diverse set of issues like gender, sexuality, social class, or any number of social locations.

Student responses demonstrated the value of the lecture via shared enjoyment and explanation of how it kept their interest which is important given common reports of student disengagement from the topic of racism. Students also shared the impact of the lesson on their perspectives of race and race relations. Reactions ranged from surprise, disappointment in themselves, to happiness in learning something about how they have been navigating through their environments. Eliciting genuine emotion and reflection led to a change in attitudes and beliefs via a connection to broader concepts. The lesson accomplishes the intended goals of facilitating student engagement with sociological concepts of race in a critical manner.

In Haddad and Lieberman's (2002) article, Berger (1963, p.175) was quoted as stating:

> Even those who do not find in this intellectual pursuit their own particular demon ... will by this contact have become a little less stolid in their prejudices, a little more careful in their own commitments and a little more skeptical about the commitments of others – and perhaps a little more compassionate in their journey through life.

This statement encompasses what I gathered from the majority of student responses. Given the powerful impact this lecture has had on their perspectives, it is my belief that this lecture could contribute to any professor's pedagogical approach. The lesson can serve as a tool that will help teach and reach students about a delicate topic. With the complexity of modern racism and student resistance to the idea of racial inequality, I am hopeful that professors will benefit from use of this lecture. Most importantly, I hope students who use this idea will gain insight into the complexity of racial attitudes in America and awaken their sociological imagination.

Note

1 A simple Google search for "Pit Bull myths" will yield this and many other commonly held myths.

Bibliography

Alexander, M., 2010. *The new Jim Crow: Mass incarceration in the age of colorblindness*. New York, NY: New Press, Inc.

American Temperament Test Society, 2013. *ATTS breed statistics*. [online] Available at: <http://atts.org/breed-statistics/statistics-page1> [Accessed 14 January 2014].

Berger, P., 1963. *Invitation to Sociology: A humanistic perspective*. New York, NY: Anchor Books.

Bohmer, S. and Briggs, J.L., 1991. Teaching privileged students about gender, race, and class oppression. *Teaching Sociology*, 19(2), pp.154–63.

Brand, D., 1987. *Time bombs on legs*, Time, 27 July p.60.

Burstein, D., 2004. Breed specific legislation: Unfair prejudice and ineffective policy. *Animal Law*, 10, pp.313–28.

Bush-Baskette, S.R., 2010. *Misguided justice: The war on drugs and the incarceration of black women*. Bloomington, IN: iUniverse, Inc.

Comstock, S., 2009. *RE: Temperament of the APBT*. [email]. Message to Paul Hernandez. Sent Wednesday 11 November 2009.

Delise, K., 2007. *The Pit Bull placebo: The media, myths and politics of canine aggression*. Ramsey, NJ: Anubis Publishing.

Entman, R.M. and Rojecki, A., 2000. *The black image in the white mind: Media and race in America*. Chicago, IL: University of Chicago Press.

Gabbidon, S.L., Higgins, G.E. and Nelson, M., 2012. Public support for racial profiling in airports: Results from a statewide poll. *Criminal Justice Policy Review*, 23(2), pp.254–69.

Gamson, W.A., 1992. *Talking politics*. New York, NY: Cambridge University Press.

Green, M., 1987. *An instinct for the kill*. People, 6 July, pp.29–31.

Haddad, A.T. and Lieberman, L., 2002. From student resistance to embracing the sociological imagination: Unmasking privilege, social conventions, and racism. *Teaching Sociology*, 30(3), pp.328–41.

Harlow, R., 2009. Innovations in teaching race and class inequality: Bittersweet candy and the vanishing dollar. *Teaching Sociology*, 37, pp.194–204.

Healey, J.F., 2010. *Race, ethnicity, gender, and class*. Los Angeles, CA: Sage Publications.

Khanna, N. and Harris, C.A., 2009. Teaching race as a social construction: Two interactive class exercises. *Teaching Sociology*, 37, pp.369–78.

National Geographic, 2009. *Bite force competition between Rottweiler, German Shepard, and Pitbull.* [online] Available at: <https://www.youtube.com/watch?v=eV MECV3za44> [Accessed 14 January 2014].

Obach, B.K., 1999. Demonstrating the social construction of race. *Teaching Sociology*, 27(3), pp.252–57.

——, 2000. Teaching about institutional discrimination and the controversies of affirmative action. *Teaching Sociology*, 28(1), pp.50–55.

Pence, D.J. and Fields, J.A., 1999. Teaching about race and ethnicity: Trying to uncover white privilege for a white audience. *Teaching Sociology*, 27(2), pp.150–58.

Rockler, N.R., 2002. Race, whiteness, "lightness," and relevance: African American and European American interpretations of Jump Start and The Boondocks. *Critical Studies in Media Communication*, 19, pp.398–418.

Swift, E.M., 1987. The Pit Bull friend and killer: Is the Pit Bull a fine animal, as its admirers claim, or is it a vicious dog, unfit for society? *Sports Illustrated*, 27 July, pp.73–84.

Time Inc., 2013. *Time.* [online] Available at: <http://www.timeinc.com/brands/news-businessfinance.php> [Accessed 14 January 2014].

Townsley, E., 2007. The social construction of social facts: Using the U.S. Census to examine race as a scientific and moral category. *Teaching Sociology*, 35, pp.223–38.

Winant, H., 2000. Race and race theory. *Annual Review of Sociology*, 26, pp.169–85.

Zatz, M., 2012. *Punishing immigrants: Policy, politics and injustice.* New York: NY, University Press.

2

RESEARCH ON TEACHING SENSITIVE TOPICS

A review of the challenges and opportunities for enhancing the classroom experience

Kathryn A. Branch and Tara N. Richards

College professors may face situations where their course curricula cover "sensitive topics" such as sexual assault, racial inequality, and child abuse where the material has the potential to personally and/or negatively affect students in the class. In our experience as professors, teaching courses that focus on sensitive topics can be challenging. We have found that many students reveal that they have personally experienced the topic discussed in the course material or that they know a friend, relative, or co-worker who has had the experience. This personal connection with material can create both problems and opportunities for teaching in higher education. In the following sections, we first discuss several of the common challenges to teaching sensitive topics (e.g., cognitive dissonance, emotional reactions to the material, and student disclosures of victimization). We then outline several strategies for enhancing students' learning and academic growth that are discussed in the academic literature, as well as, those we have personally experienced while teaching and conducting research on teaching sensitive topics.

Challenge 1: sensitive topics and cognitive dissonance

When teaching about sensitive topics, such as sexual assault, racial inequality, or child abuse, one challenge professors may face is students' resistance to accept new or different viewpoints. Faculty who teach sensitive topics often notice cognitive dissonance from their students when students are exposed to new information that conflicts with the student's personal experience, norms, and/or world view. Cognitive dissonance is when an individual finds him or herself struggling with new information that may conflict with current beliefs or old understandings (Festinger, 1957). For example, a victim advocate came into one of our victimology courses and spoke about incidences of date rape on the university campus. After the presentation the advocate was approached by a female student who said she disagreed with the advocate's description of date rape, and that instead of it being date rape, the victims had simply "made a bad choice." When encouraged to explain, the student described how she had experienced the same situation in high school that the advocate described and when she told her parents, she was told not to talk about it with anyone and that she had "just made a bad choice." The presentation forced the student to grapple with new information (the situation was a rape) given old understandings (her parents told her she had made a bad choice).

In the classroom, a personal connection to course material can influence a student's experiential reality: what he/she knows as "real" because he/she has experienced it directly (Maxfield and Babbie, 2011). Indeed, it is a teaching tactic to encourage students to think of or even share personal experiences in order to assist with the understanding and application of the course material. However, when focusing on their own or another student's personal experience, students may lose sight of the broader social context regarding the topic. In order for students to understand both the micro and macro level factors, a delicate balance must be struck between harnessing students' personal experiences and considering the breadth of the perspectives surrounding the issue.

For example when teaching about interpersonal violence, at least one student in class is usually a direct or indirect survivor of victimization given the prevalence rates for dating violence and rape/sexual assault among college populations (see Gover, et al., 2008; Shorey, et al., 2011). As feminist criminologists, we believe it is important to support student-survivors while, at the same time, creating discussions that are meaningful for students who do not have these same personal connections. However, we must also ensure that students understand that individual experiences do not represent the only experience and that there is diversity even among similar situations. That is, victims of interpersonal violence may differ among characteristics such as age, sex, race/ethnicity, and socioeconomic status. Dependent upon one's social locations, individuals will have different victimization experiences and this should also be represented in class discussions. One way to facilitate discussion of these diverse perspectives is to ask students what they think a victim *and* a perpetrator of interpersonal violence "looks like" and "acts like" and to compare and contrast the different examples provided. When we have a difficult time beginning such discussions, we find it helpful to ask about portrayals of interpersonal violence (e.g., child abuse or dating violence) in popular movies, song lyrics, or novels and then build the discussion from there (see the appendix for specific examples). These discussions often provide "teaching moments" where students are willing to meet the faculty member half way and consider a perspective that is different from their personal worldview. Anecdotally, we have been told that these discussions "opened their eyes" to the complexity of a topic (e.g., the connection between sex, gender, power, and victimization) that was not truly understood at the beginning of the semester.

Challenge 2: emotional reactions to material

A second challenge that professors may face when teaching sensitive topics is that course material may create emotional reactions from students, and in some circumstances, trigger extraordinary reactions or crises. Durfee and Rosenberg (2009) discuss the possibility of such emotional reactions to course material citing reactions ranging from shock and anger to extreme sadness. Recently we experienced a situation during a discussion of the Holocaust and presentation of a film depicting original footage of Auschwitz, where a student became visibly ill and left the classroom. This student later reported that she had to leave the room because she had become nauseous in reaction to the images depicted in the film. After class the student approached us and recounted her physical reaction to the film. We had the opportunity to listen to the student and ensure that she had safe space to debrief from the material. We also amended the syllabus to include a warning regarding the contents of the film. As faculty members who research sensitive topics, often times we become desensitized to the potential effects of seeing and discussing disturbing topics like child sex trafficking, genocide, or inmate partner victimization. We must be prepared to create a safe space for students' emotional reactions and to take time to adequately respond to them through classroom debriefings and/or one-on-one discussions after class. Further, Durfee and Rosenberg (2009) urge instructors to carefully consider the potential impact a course topic (e.g., sexual assault, murder, suicide) or course material (e.g., a video that has a scene of violence) may have on students when developing their course schedules and syllabi. Given that faculty at institutions of higher education are rarely trained to assist a student in crisis (Karjane, et al., 2002), we must coordinate with on-campus resources to ensure that we have a safety net in place for students who may benefit from assistance beyond their professor's skill or comfort level.

Challenge 3: student disclosure of victimization

A third challenge faced when teaching about sensitive topics is that classroom material may trigger a student to disclose a personal victimization experience to the professor or to the class as a whole. A survey of faculty at two U.S. universities demonstrated that student to faculty disclosures are a common occurrence and that faculty who teach sensitive topics are at an increased risk of receiving such disclosures compared to professors who do not teach sensitive topics (Richards, et al., 2013). Durfee and Rosenberg (2009) suggest that faculty who teach sensitive topics are likely to receive disclosures because students perceive them to be an "expert" (p.104) on the topic and/or that professor has already broached the topic or an equally sensitive topic in class.

Impact of disclosures on students and the classroom

Student disclosures often create a unique challenge for professors in regards to ensuring that the classroom is a safe place for all students. Rosenbloom and Fetner (2001) acknowledge that the "process of self-disclosure, both as a revelation of personal information in the classroom or between teacher and student is a social matter that affects classroom dynamics" (p.442). On one occasion, one of us received a spontaneous disclosure of child abuse during a discussion of child maltreatment in our juvenile justice class. A female student indicated that, over a period of several years, an uncle had abused her and that when she told her parents they refused to believe her. This disclosure changed the dynamic of the class discussion instantly. The classroom became quiet. Students who had directed their attention to the disclosing student quickly looked away and down at their desks. The disclosing student continued to look at the front of the classroom and, as the professor, we had to respond, quickly, but carefully. In this case, we were able to express to that student that we were sorry that they had experienced the abuse (validating their experience and demonstrating that their experience was important) and reinforce the personal disclosure by drawing on the broader literature regarding child maltreatment (e.g., prevalence of abuse by family members relative to strangers, hesitation of adults to believe children) – simultaneously contextualizing the topic for other students and validating the survivor. Durfee and Rosenberg (2009) suggest that if a student chooses to disclose (whether inside the classroom or to the faculty alone) it is important for faculty to clear a space for listening to the student, demonstrate a readiness to listen, and engage in active listening techniques. When possible, instructors should engage students in the moment of their disclosure (Durfee and Rosenberg, 2009). Indeed, when a student discloses, they must become the priority and the discussion must be crafted with the student's well-being in mind. Durfee and Rosenberg indicate that, "for many survivors who reach out to instructors, this may be the first time they have disclosed their experiences to anyone. By simply listening to students retell their lived experience, instructors help students process what has happened to them" (p.109).

Comparatively, when students receive ambivalent or openly negative reactions to their disclosures from their professors and/or other students they may be unintentionally silenced and may no longer feel comfortable sharing their experience (Konradi, 1993). In cases where classmates respond inappropriately to student disclosures, faculty must immediately address the statements in class in a firm but professional manner. For example, in one of our victimology courses, a male student made a comment that all of the rapes he knew about in his time as a military police officer were situations where the women simply "regretted having sex." In response, we acknowledged the student's point, that false reports do happen, and we promised to discuss this phenomenon in the class, but we also immediately made clear that false reports were rare and the low prevalence of false reports were documented in the empirical research. True to our word, over the course of the semester, we discussed rape myths and ensured these discussions included statistics regarding the prevalence of the false reporting of rape/sexual assault compared to other crimes. In addition, we invited a victim's advocate to speak to the class regarding the extensive personal and financial costs of being a rape victim. As a result, we ensured that all students in the class felt safe and that no one's viewpoints were dismissed, but instead, we reached the empirical "truth" regarding the topic together as a class. Underprepared faculty who inadequately respond to negative reactions to a student's disclosure by other students may inadvertently create a whole host of problems for the entire classroom community such as the inadvertent perpetuation of myths/stereotypes, victim blaming attitudes, or the revictimization of student survivors.

The effect of student disclosure on professors

In addition to the effect of disclosures on students and the classroom, researchers have also begun to explore the impact of student disclosures on professors and instructors (Hayes-Smith, et al., 2010; Branch, et al., 2011; Richards, et al., 2013). Both qualitative and quantitative data suggest that professors are affected by their student's disclosures (Branch, et al., 2011). Hayes-Smith, et al. (2010) found that 19 percent of professors in their sample reported feeling strain in negotiating their role as a professor after a student disclosure. After a student had disclosed a victimization experience, many professors reported that post-disclosure they approached the discussion of sensitive topics more carefully and struggled to balance their desire to maintain an open classroom environment with their concern for survivors' wellbeing (Hayes-Smith, et al., 2010). Additional research by Branch, et al. (2011) found that professors in their sample reported feeling concern for students after the disclosure. For example, a participant revealed, "and this is where it's hard ... It's hard because I'm doing all things via email ... sometimes telephone ... every once and a while they'll come in and speak with me. He seemed to be okay with it but I'm always concerned that they're not okay" (Branch, et al., 2011, p. 13). Faculty discussed a desire to protect the student from hostile comments made by other students in the course after a disclosure. We have personally experienced the difficulty of continuing to discuss the topic of sexual assault after learning that a student in the course was a survivor. After receiving a disclosure from a female student enrolled in one of our victimology classes, we found ourselves consistently looking at the female student throughout the discussion to ensure she was not demonstrating signs of distress and being particularly concerned about the presentation of material and classroom discussion negatively impacting her over the course of the semester.

Research also demonstrates that many professors report personally experiencing some type of negative feeling after receiving a disclosure of victimization from a student (Hayes-Smith, et al., 2010). One participant explained, "After she [the student-survivor] left I felt really angry ... angry that this keeps happening to college women. I found myself walking around campus and being angry and wondering if one of the young men that I taught had committed this assault ... it is hard for me to not think about their stories when I go home at night" (Hayes-Smith, et al., 2010, p.14). Another professor stated, "I mean there was a period ... there was a semester when I was having nightmares because you know I was carrying their stories home with me. It was this real emotional burden for me at times" (Hayes-Smith, et al., 2010, p.14). These results emphasize the importance of self-care for faculty members who teach sensitive topics. Instructors may find it helpful to debrief after receiving a student disclosure (while keeping the student's identity confidential). In our own experience we have found the practice of sharing the weight of student disclosures with trusted colleagues personally helpful. In addition, we have found Martin's perspectives on self-care in the text, *Rape Work* (2005), a wonderful source of information.

It is also important to note that professors must still serve the role of teacher after a disclosure of victimization. A professor's role can become complicated when a student discloses in an assignment where one has to be an objective grader but also does not want to further traumatize the student-victim (Branch, et al., 2011). Specifically, faculty may find it difficult to critique a student's writing format/style and/or to give a student a poor grade on an assignment that includes a disclosure of victimization. In grading such assignments, faculty must be clear as to the aim of their critiques (e.g., citations, format, quality of writing). When we receive an assignment that includes a disclosure, no matter what grade the student has earned, we find it helpful to give back these assignments at the end of class and take time to personally and privately explain the grading to the student.

Another important consideration regarding student to faculty disclosures is whether or not faculty are obligated to report student disclosures of crime victimization under the "Clery Act." The Jeanne Clery Disclosure of Campus Security Police and Campus Crime Statistics Act is a federal law enacted by Congress in 1990[1] that requires U.S. institutions of higher education, both public and private, that participate in federal student aid programs to disclose crime statistics for the campus and make timely warnings of criminal activities. In regards to reporting specifically, one of the Clery Act's provisions indicates that universities must develop "policies which encourage accurate and prompt reporting of all crimes to the campus police and the appropriate law enforcement agencies" (Jeanne Clery Act, 2008, n.p.). Thus, the Clery Act provides general expectations regarding an institution's duty to compile and report crimes perpetrated on campus and/or that include students off campus but leaves institutions free to develop their own specific processes and procedures. In an attempt to comply with the Clery Act, anecdotally we understand that some institutions require that institutional officials with significant responsibility for campus and student activities (which may include all faculty, faculty who serve as advisors to student groups or coaches, and/or staff involved in student affairs) to report disclosures of crime victimization. As a result, at some institutions, if a professor receives a disclosure of crime victimization from a student they are required to report the crime to administrators – even if the student does not want to report the crime. Comparatively, some institutions (e.g., Vanderbilt University) require faculty to report their knowledge of crimes on campus but allow faculty to report the incident without revealing the identity of the victim. Therefore, faculty should consult their own faculty handbooks to determine their institution's interpretation of the Clery Act. Upon inspection of their university's reporting procedures, individual faculty may uncover victim-centered problems with the processes and recognize opportunities to provide professional guidance to their university in regards to modifying or augmenting procedures.

Innovations in teaching pedagogies

College faculty from across the social sciences have developed innovative teaching pedagogies for use in classes covering sensitive topics such as race and crime, rape/sexual assault, ethnic genocide, and child abuse which have been disseminated in peer reviewed journals and through professional organizations. Specific examples of resources such as texts and films are included in the appendix. For example, Murphy-Geiss (2008) suggests that, "the traditional instruction models of reading and lecture are not appropriate when teaching a course on the issue of domestic violence. Instead, attention should be paid to multiple pedagogies that highlight emotionally engaging methods and realistic situations" (p.385). Specific classroom strategies detailed below include the use of course readings, films, assignments, community engagement/ personal observations (e.g., domestic violence courts), and guest speakers. Also, procedural practices such as trigger warnings, alternative assignments, and a list of resources in the course syllabus can assist instructors in facilitating sensitive topics in the classroom.

Readings

Instructors have multiple options when deciding what readings and texts to include in a class on sensitive topics: qualitative, quantitative, ethnographies, first-person accounts, or "readers" and/or a mixture of different types of readings (see the appendix for specific resources). Several scholars have also independently identified reading resources that have worked well within their own classes. For example, Gardner (1993) asserts the importance of choosing "materials that provide a strong conceptual framework for analyzing domestic violence yet, at the same time, do not objectify those who have experienced it" (p.96). In her experience, qualitative texts work best to meet these goals and she recommends classic texts such as *Violence against Wives* by Emerson Dobash and Russell Dobash (1992) and *Father-Daughter Incest* by Judith Herman (2000). Comparatively, Gardner (1993) found quantitative texts "did little to increase students' understanding of the dynamics or social context of violent behavior, and this was especially true for those who had not directly experienced violence" (p.96). Gardner found that student-survivor feedback regarding quantitative texts were consistently negative with some student-survivors reporting "feeling re-victimized and objectified by texts" that were "unreal" and "lifeless" (Gardner, 1993, p.96). Murphy-Geiss (2008) suggests that it is "essential to include intentionally controversial readings" in classes on domestic violence so that students will engage in discussions and debates regarding the many difficult issues surrounding the problem of domestic violence (e.g., why don't victims just leave?).[2]

Gardner (1993) also lauds the use of first person narrative accounts of gendered victimization such as *Voices in the Night* (1982), edited by Toni McNaron and Yarrow Morgan, and *I Never Told Anyone* (1991), edited by Ellen Bass and Louise Thornton while Hollander (2005) suggests *On Becoming a Dangerous Woman* (1992) by Elena Featherston and *Poem About My Rights* (1980) by June Jordan. Such first person accounts serve several purposes. For survivors in the course, they may "validate and affirm their own victimization experiences" (Gardner, 1993, p.97), while at the same time, assisting other students in the course in "gaining a deeper understanding of what it means to be victimized" (p.97). However, Gardner warns that personal narratives, which often include graphic descriptions of victimization experiences, may trigger negative feelings and/or inadvertently re-victimize survivors. As such, students should be adequately prepared for the subject matter included in the texts (e.g., through either the syllabus or in-class discussions or both) and instructors must be vigilant in their observation of signs of student problems during class discussions of the readings and/or assignments on the readings. Likewise, such readings might be included in the course as "optional" reading or instructors might provide alternative readings for students depending on the comfort level of the instructor.

Films

Instructors may also use films as instructional aids when teaching about sensitive topics. A film can be used to create interest in a sensitive topic, to personalize a sensitive topic, to provide visual imagery for visual learners, to reinforce content from class discussion, and/or to create critical discussion and debate. Film can influence the way students see things and as a result faculty must be thoughtful in their choice of film. Similar to the selection of other course materials (e.g., PowerPoints, readings, and guest presentations), film selection needs to be conducted in a thoughtful, planned and purposeful manner that is integrative with course materials and objectives. Effective integration of film into classroom instruction involves planning and preparation before the film (e.g., giving students background about the film and purposes for showing it), during the film (e.g., giving students a specific task during the film like looking for class concepts in the film), and after the students view the film (e.g., having students complete a critical analysis of the film and having a class discussion). We have consistently used, *Sentencing the Victim* (2002) a film that follows a rape victim through the process of prosecuting her victimizers as a tool to reinforce lectures on rape/sexual assault. This film affords viewers an inside look at how the crime of rape effects both primary victims *and* secondary victims such as friends and family. We show this film directly after our discussion of the prevalence of rape/sexual assault and myths about false reporting. We provide students with questions to consider as we watch and we pause the film to discuss these points periodically. In the subsequent class period, we bring in a victim's advocate to finish our coverage of the topic.

Course assignments

Extant literature provides multiple course assignments that may serve as effective tools for combatting the previously outlined challenges encountered when teaching sensitive topics. Assignments include group work such as in-class group discussions, social change projects, and policy evaluations. Individual level assignments include media analyses, structured journaling, and free writing assignments.

Gardner (1993) indicates several assignments that have been especially successful in her course on domestic violence: (1) in-class discussion groups and (2) student-initiated social-change projects. She asserts that "both activities help to create a sense of community within the classroom and they also provide time for students to talk with each other about their thoughts, feelings, and reactions to the course" (p.98). Gardner suggests that instructors may choose to use student-initiated social-change projects in lieu of the traditional term paper. For social-change projects, students are grouped together by their interests into groups of four to six. Student groups are then asked to develop a proposal and submit it to the instructor for review and constructive commentary. Once the proposal is approved, the instructor helps facilitate linkages between the student groups and campus and/or community organizations. Gardner asserts that in her class on domestic violence, these assignments offer students an avenue to "translate their anger and frustration regarding the prevalence of domestic violence into concrete social action designed to reduce it" (p.99). Examples of projects that have been successful in our own classrooms include participation in a university-wide awareness day, a role in the university's Take Back the Night event, or the presentation of workshops in residence halls or at campus clubs/organizations on such topics as child abuse, dating violence, or self-defense strategies.

In her class on violence against women, Hollander (2005) uses class assignments to not only reinforce important aspects of such violence but also to encourage students to think about social change and resistance to violence. After the course discussion of rape and sexual assault, students work in teams to evaluate their campus's existing sexual assault prevention strategies and develop ideas for improving campus resources. Students complete a media analysis assignment where they first investigate representations of violence against women in the media and then search for alternative representations of women's empowerment and safety.

Finally, free writing and/or journaling assignments may also assist in teaching sensitive topics. Konradi (1993) suggests asking students to "write off the top of their heads" in response to the readings and/or lecture material. Students' responses can then be used to facilitate class discussion where students can both share their own opinions and questions with the class as well as respond to others. Instructors might also assign students journal-writing exercises over the course of the semester (Lee, 1989). For example, instructors might have a structured set of response questions for students to reflect and write on or students might simply keep a log of their thoughts and feelings about the topics covered in the course. By journaling, students keep an ongoing log and have the opportunity to assess changes in their opinions regarding course topics and/or policies as the class progresses.

Community events and guest speakers

Lee (1989) suggests utilizing community events pertaining to class topics to bring class material to life. Specifically, Lee indicates that she provides students the opportunity to earn class credit for attending community or on-campus events that are relevant to class topics. For example, students might attend a community or on-campus Take Back the Night, a lecture by non-violence activists such as Men Against Rape, or a poetry reading sponsored by the campus Women's Center.

Murphy-Geiss (2008) describes how one of her pedagogical strategies is for students in a class on domestic violence to observe domestic violence court. She contends that, "there is no classroom equivalent, even through powerful films and guest presentations, that can create the effect of actually seeing and hearing a woman with a broken arm and black eye request that the judge return her husband to the home, reporting that it was just an accident" (p.381). She freely admits that not every student will see such a dramatic court event but that each student will observe a situation that will bring the lectures, readings, and films to life. As the instructor, Murphy-Geiss worked with campus service learning to facilitate the partnership with a local domestic violence court. In her experience, the court welcomed her students and even utilized them to collect observational data for court personnel. Murphy-Geiss suggests several other strategies for creating such partnerships including working with a local domestic violence organization and/or contacting the court directly to gain entrance for her students. Such service learning opportunities require some planning and flexibility (see Murphy-Geiss, 2008 for observation guides and schedules) on the part of the instructor but provide unique and meaningful learning experiences for students.

In the case of teaching violent victimization such as child abuse, domestic violence, and/or rape/sexual assault faculty may bring survivors of violence into the classroom as guest speakers. Such "authoritative knowers" may provide students with personal anecdotes about experiencing violence that will bring the course material to life as well as tangible examples of how victimization may be transformed into avenues for self-empowerment (Lee, 1989; Hollander, 2005). Gardner (1993) asserts that appropriate guest speakers elicit positive feedback from students in her course on domestic violence. She finds that students note, "how the speakers' personal stories made many of the concepts and issues of the course 'come to life' and enabled them to stop 'blaming the victim'" (p.98). Instructors may also consider inviting victim's advocates into the classroom to reinforce classroom lectures and link students to local resources. Information on successful local and/or national social action campaigns (e.g., One Student, Red Flag, Take Back the Night) also provides students with tangible examples of the scope of the problem of violence as well as the spectrum of support for combating such violence. In our own victimology class, we have invited a guest speaker from the local crisis center to speak to the class about rape and sexual assault. This speaker shared information with students about the local resources available in the community and also shared her personal experience as a rape survivor. Her story included a discussion of the challenges she experienced with the criminal justice system after the rape. This revelation provided a fantastic teaching moment for students, given that earlier that semester, we discussed the concept of victim blaming and the second assault that many victims report experiencing at the hands of the criminal justice system. Students reported in their course evaluations that the speaker's personal story helped them integrate and humanize/personalize the concepts discussed in class.

Procedural practices

Procedural practices also provide powerful tools for teaching sensitive topics in the classroom. A syllabus may provide a "warning" to students that the class focuses on a sensitive topic and provide "ground rules" for class discussions (Konradi, 1993; Durfee and Rosenberg, 2009). Instructors may read and explain this section of the syllabus to students on the first day of class so that students have a "roadmap" for the course and may make an informed choice concerning their ability to handle the class material (Konradi, 1993). In our own syllabi we include both a student professionalism policy indicating expectations of students (e.g., *students will be respectful of others' opinions and cultures*) as well as faculty professionalism statements that articulate what students may expect from us as faculty (e.g., *the faculty member seeks to facilitate the classroom experience in an academically honest and ethical way and will conduct lectures and discussions in a respectful manner*). In addition, syllabi can provide contact numbers for on-campus resources as well as local off-campus counseling or crisis centers (Lee, 1989; Gardner, 1993; Konradi, 1993; Durfee and Rosenberg, 2009); in our opinion, syllabi for courses focused on sensitive topics should include contact numbers for resources so that students may easily and privately, contact resources if they so choose.

Konradi (1993) also indicates the importance of student and faculty introductions as well as learning names in a class on sensitive topics. Konradi asserts that, "To call a person by name is to acknowledge her or him as a person" (p.19). She suggests that using names during class discussions assists in building community in the classroom and promotes the validation of individuals' ideas and experiences. Allowing time for introductions at the beginning of the course may assist students in identifying similarities between themselves such as home states, majors, and/or campus clubs or organizations and encourage a sense of camaraderie in the classroom. Such activities will help promote the classroom as a safe space where students can share their ideas and opinions.

Finally, faculty should provide an opportunity for students to "debrief" after they are presented with sensitive topics in class lectures or via guest speakers and/or videos. The faculty member may conduct a debriefing session or instructors may request that a representative from the on-campus advocacy and/or counseling center debrief the class. In these sessions, students should have the opportunity to be heard, to express their opinions and concerns regarding the material presented, as well as to ask lingering questions regarding the topic at hand. Instructors/staff who lead debriefing sessions should make an attempt to provide students with information that will assist them in developing internal resolution regarding the course material. For example, in our classes, after a presentation on rape and sexual assault, students are provided with information regarding resources for victims and perpetrators as well as information concerning prevention and intervention programs by the public health and criminal justice systems. We make every effort to remain aware of students who seem especially negatively impacted by class presentations on sensitive topics (e.g., students who express physical distress or are overly emotive or combative). In response to such students, we have utilized a range of options from talking to the student one-on-one to providing them with physical materials regarding counseling services (which we bring with us to the classroom for each victimology course meeting).

Conclusions

In this chapter we began with a discussion of the challenges of teaching sensitive topics including the negative reactions of students to course material, student disclosures of personal experiences, and the impact of student disclosures on professors, students, and the classroom community as a whole. We also presented resources as well as procedural practices that may help facilitate an engaging, safe, and hospitable teaching/learning environment for courses on sensitive topics. However, the resources presented here are by no means an exhaustive list of strategies and materials available for faculty. Many professional listservs as well as websites for community advocates, nonprofits, and governmental organizations provide avenues for sharing up-to-date lists of readings, films, and community events that are relevant for courses covering sensitive topics. Indeed, open dialog and collaboration among professors and practitioners in the field is key to ensuring that courses on sensitive topics produce the most powerful and memorable learning experiences for our students.

Appendix

Popular media examples

Movies: *Kids, Freeway, Girl with the Dragon Tattoo, Sleepers, The Perks of Being a Wallflower,* and *Monster.*

Songs: "Keep Your Head Up" (Tupac Shakur), "Janie's Got a Gun" (Aerosmith), "Polly" (Nirvana), "Hands Clean" (Alanis Morissette), "Animal" (Pearl Jam), and "Date Rape" (Sublime).

Books: *Room* (Emma Donoghue), *The Lovely Bones* (Alice Sebold), *The Perks of Being a Wildflower* (Stephen Chbosky), *Push* (Sapphire), and *The Color Purple* (Alice Walker).

Additional film recommendations

Some examples of films for teaching sensitive topics include the classic documentary *Defending our Lives*, a 1993 film that tells the stories of four women who are in prison for killing their batterers. In addition, Murphy-Geiss (2008) suggests *Terror at Home: Domestic Violence in America*, a 2005 film which recounts the stories of seven different women as they attempt to escape violent partners. *The Invisible War* (2012) provides a detailed account of rape and sexual assault in the military as well as the barriers victims face in their pursuit of prosecution. In addition, *A Family Affair* (2010) offers a powerful picture of familial child abuse and maltreatment as well as the effects of such abuse on adult survivors; *Bully* (2012) delivers a detailed account of bullying in school, the consequences of bullying, and the reaction of teachers and parents to bullying behavior.

Notes

1 It was first enacted by the US Congress in 1990 and amended in 1992, 1998, 2000, and 2010.
2 See Loseke, Gelles, and Cavanaugh's (2005) edited volume, *Current Controversies on Family Violence,* for an example of intentionally controversial readings.

Bibliography

Bass, E. and Thornton, L. eds., 1991. *I never told anyone.* New York: HarperCollins.
Branch, K., Hayes-Smith, B. and Richards, T., 2011. Professors' experiences with student disclosures of sexual assault and intimate partner violence: How "helping" students can inform teaching practices. *Feminist Criminology,* 6(1), pp.54–75.
Dobash, E. and Dobash, R., 1992. *Violence against wives.* New York, NY: Routledge.

Durfee, A. and Rosenberg, K., 2009. Teaching sensitive issues: Feminist pedagogy and the practice of advocacy-based counseling. *Feminist Teacher*, 19(2), pp.103–21.

Featherston, E., 1992. On becoming a dangerous woman. In: A. Sumrall and D. Taylor, eds., *Sexual harassment: Women speak out*. Freedom, CA: Crossing Press. pp.71–77.

Festinger, L., 1957. *A theory of cognitive dissonance*. Stanford: Stanford University Press.

Gardner, S., 1993. Teaching about domestic violence: Strategies for empowerment. *NWSA Journal*, 5(1), pp.94–102.

Gover, A., Kaukinen, C. and Fox, K., 2008. The relationship between violence in the family of origin and dating violence among college students. *Journal of Interpersonal Violence*, 23, pp.1667–93.

Hayes-Smith, R., Richards, T. and Branch, K., 2010. " … but I'm not a counselor:" The nature of role strain experienced by female professors when a student discloses sexual assault and intimate partner violence. ELiSS, 2(3), pp.1756–1848X.

Herman, J., 2000. *Father-daughter incest*. Cambridge, MA: Harvard.

Hollander, J., 2005. Challenging despair: Teaching about women's resistance to violence. *Violence Against Women*, 11(6), pp.776–91.

Jeanne Clery Act, 2008. *Jeanne Clery Disclosure of Campus Security Policy and Campus Crime Statistics Act*. [online] Available at: <http://clerycenter.org/node/38> [12 December 2013].

Jordan, J., 1980. Poem about my rights. In *Passion: New poems*. Boston: Beacon. pp.85–88.

Karjane, H., Fisher, B. and Cullen, F., 2002. *Campus sexual assault: How America's institutions of higher education respond*. (NCJ 196676). Washington, DC: National Institute of Justice.

Keating, B., 1998. *Resource material for teaching about family violence*. Washington, DC: American Sociological Association.

Konradi, A., 1993. Teaching about sexual assault: Problematic silences and solutions. *Teaching Sociology*, 21(1), pp.13–25.

Lee, J., 1989. Our hearts are collectively breaking: Teaching survivors about violence. *Gender & Society*, 3(4), pp.541–48.

Loseke, D.R., Gelles, R.J. and Cavanaugh, M.M., 2005. *Current controversies on family violence*. Thousand Oaks, CA: Sage.

Martin, P.Y., 2005. *Rape work*. New York: Routledge.

Maxfield, M. and Babbie, E., 2011. *Research methods for criminal justice and criminology*. 6th ed. Belmont: Wadsworth, Cengage Learning.

McNaron, T. and Morgan, Y. eds., 1982. *Voices in the night*. San Francisco: Cleis Press.

Murphy-Geiss, G., 2008. Bringing the facts to life: Facilitating student engagement with the issue of domestic violence. *Teaching Sociology*, 36(4), pp.378–88.

Richards, T., Branch, K. and Hayes, R., 2013. An exploratory examination of college student to professor disclosures of crime victimization. *Violence Against Women*, 19(11), pp.1408–22.

Rosenbloom, S. and Fetner, T., 2001. Sharing secrets slowly: Issues of classroom self-disclosure raised by student sex workers. *Teaching Sociology,* 29(4), pp.439–53.

Sentencing the Victim, 2002 [DVD]. *Sentencing the Victim* IVS Video, Inc.

Shorey, R., Stuart, G. and Cornelius, T., 2011. Dating violence and substance use in college students: A review of the literature. *Aggression and Violent Behavior,* 16, pp.541–50.

3

SELF-REFLECTION IN MOTION

The victimology classroom

Helen Jones

This chapter will discuss the particular challenges related to teaching victimology including student/educator power relations, student disclosures and why students sometimes turn to victim-blaming. Asking "why" is a very good starting point. Of course there is a danger of seeking a "one-size-fits-all" solution and ending up with something that might be illuminating yet partial. Rather than seek a single answer, we can accept that answers will be multifaceted, messy and, at times, mind expanding. For over two decades I have taught victimology to students studying sociology, criminology, social policy and law, at undergraduate and postgraduate levels in the United Kingdom. Most students demonstrate amazing depths of empathy and understanding but one or two can derail a class. It is to those instances, where teaching a sensitive topic is made more difficult, that this chapter is focused.

The aim is not merely to propose *what* might be taught through the content of a victimology class, although examples and suggestions for best practice will be given. Rather the emphasis is on *how* it might be taught. How can we engage students to think beyond their own experience, to question their own beliefs, to identify their assumptions and to even challenge their own biases?

The first portion of the chapter provides a definition of victimology and outlines the types of topics that are covered in these classes. I also discuss the demography of the classroom because understanding our students is the first step in developing a reflective pedagogy. The second section considers the pedagogic sensitivities and challenges surrounding how we teach victimology. Some of us shun the notion of pedagogy. It can seem abstract and difficult: why do we need to learn about philosophies of education? Others find it applicable and easy: educating is what we do and implementing our philosophy is part of why we do it. Knowing is different than doing. In complex modern times, characterized by socio-political change, many educators have drawn on practices that are concerned with social difference and social transformation to engage students and foster social justice. Therefore, a critical pedagogy is necessary. This approach allows for the teacher to acknowledge their own limitations. It also allows for the authenticity of student experience to be acknowledged and shows how both educator and student can learn together. The final section takes a practical turn to offering tactics and strategies to be used in the classroom. A couple of example exercises are offered to complement other examples provided elsewhere in this book.

What is victimology?

Victimology is an area of study concerned with victims, offenders, criminal justice systems, rights movements and power. Its theoretical history lies in the work of von Hentig (1948), Mendelsohn (1963), Karmen (1992) and many others who have written about the connections between crime, harm and justice. The subject matter of victimology can be local and intimate, or global and include torture, terrorism and war. These are complicated issues on which people often hold strong opinions based on their own experiences, interests and values. There are no easy answers. The number of universities offering victimology courses has increased over the last twenty years (Dussich, 2006) and scholarship on victimology is well established, with a number of explicitly dedicated journals, including *International Review of Victimology* and *International Perspectives in Victimology*. Examples of typical syllabi are included in the Division on Women and Crime's Teaching

Resources and cover the theories and methods that have emerged from the disciplines of sociology and criminology. Victimization topics, such as intimate partner abuse, child abuse and workplace and prisons, are often covered. The subject matter of victimology takes us as educators into sensitive areas and much has been written about the relevance of emotion in the classroom when teaching such topics and the need to develop different models of teaching to encourage mutual respect and self-reflectivity (hooks, 1994; Fisher, 2001; Lowe and Jones, 2010). Taught well, the dynamic of the victimology classroom has much to offer courses that fall outside of its remit as the intersection between disciplinary context and pedagogic practice creates a context for dialogue which can be conceptualized as "self-reflection in motion." We journey with our students into places of which they may have no prior knowledge: the abuser, the drug user, the fraudster, the exploiter and the thief. Alternatively, they may have far more experience of these worlds than us, and for them education may be a route out of these worlds.

Who are the students in our classrooms and what demographics might be shared with the "typical" victim? If we look for a moment at the data from victim surveys, we find that victims of street violence tend to be young men, victims of sexual violence tend to be young women and victims of hate crimes tend to be ethnic minority populations (Truman and Planty, 2011). According to a 2012 survey (American College Health Association, 2013), 11 percent of male college level students had been in a physical fight in the previous 12 months, 10 percent of female students had been in an emotionally abusive relationship, and five percent of all students had experienced some form of discrimination. Now lift your gaze to the students sitting before you. Do they fit the profile of these victims? Our students tend to fall into categories most likely to be affected by crime. They also come from a range of ethnic backgrounds and they often comprise a wide range of identities which are not as easily read as age, gender and ethnicity, which include sexuality, economic and political diversity.

So we may have victims of crime sitting in front of us. They may be survivors of past experiences but they might also be experiencing ongoing victimization. We may also have perpetrators in our class. If we know who the victims and villains are, do we treat them differently? Do we don the white gloves to treat the victims as delicately as we would cut-glass crystal, fearful that they may break by facing the uncomfortable subject matter which for them has been a lived reality? Do we get tough with the tough guys? Can we tailor our teaching practice to accommodate the possibility that our classrooms contain victims and perpetrators? Educators are not, indeed should not be, therapists or law enforcement experts. But we do need to teach responsibly and sensitively about victims of crime.

What do you do when a student discloses an experience of being a victim of crime? It is a common occurrence and although it might be about something which is in the past and that they have personally resolved, for the wider group it may be unsettling at the least. One of your students might disclose that they have been the victim of burglary or some other property related crime. In such instances, and if the student is not exhibiting signs of current trauma, it might be appropriate to draw this into the class discussion, but be cautious not to use the disclosure as an opportunistic or voyeuristic case study. Because of the disciplinary nature of victimology, it is not uncommon for students to disclose experiences of sexual and intimate partner violence. In some of these cases students may speak before thinking through the consequences of disclosure. It is your job as the educator to ensure they do not get drawn into saying more than they are comfortable with and it is also your job to ensure that the class is not sidetracked by the disclosure. Acknowledging their experience by saying something like, "These are hard issues to deal with, thanks for sharing" or "We can talk further about this after the session" demonstrates that you hear what the student has said and also provides you with the space to move the discussion on if necessary.

Some years ago during a victimology session on street crime, one of the male students in the group disclosed that he had once been a member of a gang. This student, I will call him Jim, was mid-30s, white, smartly dressed, quietly spoken and professional in his demeanor. During the discussion, Jim had been nodding at the points being made but had not contributed to the class discussion. Very quietly Jim raised his hand and said "I once hospitalized a man." All eyes were on him as he disclosed that he had been part of a gang in his youth and had frequently participated in street fights. "We weren't a bad gang," Jim added. "We didn't have knives or anything but we would take on other gangs in our local area. One time I beat up a homeless guy and stood with my friends on the street corner while we watched an ambulance take him away." The other students were stunned and I was mentally running through my own personal checklist for the best way to respond. There is little pedagogical literature to assist the educator in this type of situation. I was fortunate because Jim was clear about this disclosure and continued in his typically quiet manner, "I'm not saying this so you can all judge me. I'm a different person now than I was then. I'm not saying this so that I can say I'm an expert on street crime. I'm not. But I just wanted to say this because these issues are real and they don't just affect people 'out there'. They affect us too." Jim's disclosure had a huge impact on the class. I asked if he was comfortable talking about this further. His response was that he would not have raised it if he was not prepared to talk. A sea of hands went up and not one of those students blamed or censured Jim. I took my role to be one of a simple facilitator, ensuring that everyone who wanted to speak got their chance and maintaining eye contact with Jim to ensure he was not out of his depth. As a class we moved on to talk about the importance of confidentiality in facilitating open debate and the students drew up a set of ground rules around this to help inform future discussions. That cohort of students and I taught each other a lot about dealing with disclosures in the classroom.

One issue that often arises is victim-blaming behavior, which is also discussed in Chapter 2 by Branch and Richards. Within the classroom your students might blame victims of property crime for taking insufficient security precautions in the home or they might criticize young people who are victimized on the street for lifestyle choices which mean they are out late at night, hanging out in groups or drinking alcohol. Additionally members of immigrant groups may be blamed because of stereotypical views about what is acceptable behavior within certain cultural groups. One crime which received an inordinate amount of victim blaming is rape (Eigenberg and Garland, 2008).

Victim-blaming in the context of violence against women has a rich history (Borkenhagen, 1975; Stampler, 2011). Women are frequently subjected to victim-blaming attitudes and many victims will internalize blame (Jones and Cook, 2008). We live in a society where highly sexualized images of women co-exist alongside reports of violence against women (Berrington and Jones, 2002; Anastasio and Costa, 2004) and the tacit assumption is that women bring it on themselves, that they ask for trouble and that this contributes to a cultural tolerance of sexual violence (Cowan, 2000, p.238).

Exploring students' understanding of a topic can expose victim-blaming attitudes. During a discussion on sexual harassment, my class considered a case where an employer was making unwanted sexual advances toward a female employee. The purpose was to discuss the consequences of the employee either quitting the job or reporting to the police. A student, I'll call her Joanne, said "The silly cow. She should just give him a slap and tell him to behave himself." Many in the class laughed at this and it seemed to inject humor into a possibly heavy session. In fairness, Joanne had verbalized what a number of students had been thinking but Joanne's comment was problematic. Her comment expressed an attitude which placed responsibility on the victim of the harassment and was therefore victim-blaming. What options does the teacher of such a class have before her? I could have simply rejected her comment, told her she was wrong and moved on to my next point. I could have replied by reiterating the purpose of the session (which was comparing the consequences of the victim quitting her job or reporting to the police). Sometimes we do not have the time to turn these moments into teaching moments. Sometimes it feels easier to simply reject the student's comments and sometimes we can feel out of our depth or intimidated, fearing we will make difficult situations worse. It is at these moments that we have the chance to make a difference and open minds to alternative analyses. I was fortunate that Joanne's comment came at the beginning of the class session because we had the time to really untangle the comment and create a rich learning opportunity from it. Instead of entering into a power struggle between the two of us, I opened the debate to the class and together we were able to turn this into a discussion of the potential consequences of acting with violence to sexual harassment. Joanne's throw-away comment about hitting the harasser, which was perhaps underpinned by her limited understanding of the topic, gave the whole class an opportunity to talk about victims fighting back, the risks of this and the support agencies that might help people in this situation.

Alongside creating a supportive environment for learning, educators also need to know how to avoid contributing to victimization through the materials we use and ways in which we manage the reactions of others. I have a pack of support agency leaflets and flyers which often prove useful but other, less obvious material can be useful in stimulating debate. For example, I have a photograph, taken from a magazine, of Diana Princess of Wales. In it she is wearing a short-ish skirt, dark hose and spike-heeled shoes. Students are given the lower half of the photograph and I use a "Think, Pair, Share" approach to get students to look at the photograph, pair up with another student to construct a story about the photograph and then feedback to the class. Many students will construct a story about a prostituted woman or of a woman in danger travelling home after an evening at a nightclub. Of course they then receive the top half of the photograph. The point of the exercise is to open up a space to talk about a sensitive issue and also to consider the partial judgments we all make using partial information. Although it would be nonsense to attempt to control every aspect of the classroom, it is a wise teacher who knows her or his students and can get them talking critically.

A pedagogy for victimology

Teaching with sensitivity to *who* is in our classroom can remind us to teach with sensitivity about *what* we teach and *how* we teach and this can have long reaching impacts. Learning about victimization can develop empathy in our students which may have an impact on their treatment of victims in society. Sending knowledgeable graduates into law enforcement, to work in the courts and in areas of victim assistance can impact practice and the wider system of processing crime. Fox and Cook (2011) have conducted one of the few research studies on the impact on students of studying a victimology course. They looked at student perceptions of the blameworthiness of crime victims, comparing these students with others enrolled in other courses. Their findings "suggest that the victimology students were significantly less likely to blame victims" (p.3407). Such research is useful in understanding the impact of victimology courses on students but it does not set out the pedagogy for how this is achieved.

Fox and Cook are reflective of this potential flaw in their methodology acknowledging that three different instructors no doubt employed different styles of teaching but the research does not delve into this area. Previous studies concerning teaching styles (Carmody and Washington, 2001; Nickoli, et al., 2003) suggest that the way in which the teaching is delivered is of crucial importance because mere information transfer is unlikely to affect attitude change (Malkin and Stake, 2004). Currier and Carlson (2009) argue the length of class time taken to discuss topics of victimization is instrumental in effecting attitudinal change. Yet is knowledge transmission and length of exposure to that knowledge sufficient?

Educational theorists, such as Schon (1983), have focused on the development of reflective practice. The purpose of reflection in general is to learn from an experience and Schon's arguments, subsequently taken up by others (e.g., Larrivee, 2000; Finlay and Gough, 2003; Loughran, 2006), suggest professional practice amongst educators is complex, unpredictable and messy. In order to teach the sensitive topics that emerge within victimology, professionals must be able to do more than follow set procedures; in the practice of critical reflection, they must develop the ability to examine judgments, assumptions and expectations.

Within research, there exists a sensitivity spectrum relating to crime victimization and ethical dilemmas can emerge at any stage of the research process (Lowe and Jones, 2010). University research ethics committees make many demands over social science research and scrutinize research methodologies in an effort to protect research participants. Researchers are required to take steps to inform and protect participants, yet there is little to no institutional oversight of teaching. As discussed earlier, the prevalence of crime victimization in society means that there is a high likelihood that every classroom contains survivors who might want or need to disclose. It is therefore our responsibility as educators to teach with sensitivity.

Effective teachers need to possess more than discipline knowledge (Shulman, 1986), they also need pedagogical knowledge. Sometimes this form of knowledge is often not well articulated, but teachers' understanding of pedagogy is an important aspect of successful learning and can itself be learned (Bain, 2004). A critical pedagogy for victimology would require the incorporation of a broad range of sociological dimensions already discussed in this chapter and book, including attention to gender, race, class, physical ability and sexual orientation. A constructivist approach, where meaning is constructed by the student and not simply imparted by the educator, is appropriate to the study of victimology. Knowledge transmission from educator to student is just not adequate to the job of developing critical awareness and reflection. The delivery of a didactic, 50-minute lecture, involving only transmission of information, is an ineffective way to facilitate learning. Contact time with students is precious and this approach puts me in mind of the Benjamin Franklin saying "Tell me and I forget, teach me and I may remember, involve me and I learn." A simple device I use with students is to "flip" the classroom (Bergman and Sams, 2012). This requires students to read a chapter or watch a video or listen to a podcast in their own time and in the class we spend the time on concept engagement. During this time they are asked to take responsibility for their own learning by ensuring their discussions include all elements of what I have coined a PEERS approach:

P – make your **P**oint to your peers about the subject under debate
E – **E**xplain it so that your peers understand
E – provide **E**vidence from theoretical literature or case material
R – express yourself with **R**espect for your peers
S – be ready for when someone says "**S**o what?"

This requirement for active involvement by the student does not mean an abdication of responsibility by the educator but it does constitute a critique of the "banking" model of education where the educator is seen as an all-knowing depositor of knowledge. Inspired in part by Freire (1970), bell hooks (2003) has argued that teachers must be actively involved in, and committed to, the process of self-actualization if they are to teach in a manner that empowers students. This is not easy as such pedagogy requires attention to emotions and feelings as a way of constructing a sense of community in the classroom. hooks pioneered a culturally relevant, transgressive education for social justice. Her interest lay in the interlacing dynamics of ethnicity, gender, culture and class and how this related to the whole person. Although it is inevitable that some students will have strong reactions to the topics of a victimology class, there are a number of elements for ensuring a critical pedagogy:

Know your students. Earlier in this chapter it was noted that our students often inhabit categories most likely to be affected by crime. They come from a range of ethnic backgrounds and they comprise a wide range of identities. You cannot know in advance what your students have experienced in their lives before joining your class, but you can be mindful of the possibility that they have prior knowledge (and even lived experience) of the topics covered in the course. This tacit acknowledgement is the beginning of a trust which they will value whether they disclose to you or not.

Establish group standards. This requires that you acknowledge everyone has rights and responsibilities. You have responsibilities to include statements in your course documentation outlining expectations about students' involvement, forewarning students about the explicit nature of the course and providing resources for students who may want to seek support. Their responsibilities include active participation in student-led class exercises on writing ground rules. Through this process you can refuse to be "the expert," disrupt power dynamics and start the journey towards critical consciousness.

Ensure the content is appropriate. To be relevant it has to be current and should not contain victim-blaming material, objectify victims or misrepresent marginalized groups.

Delivery style is crucial. Do not preach but find an approach which is authentic and true. Part of this quest for authenticity will be achieved by including guest talks from local law enforcement, victim advocates and other community agencies.

Find time for your students to talk with you outside of class time but be careful to establish boundaries. Remember you are not their friend; you are an educational professional. Students often reach out to instructors in the belief that they are "the expert" or because that instructor has managed to break a taboo through class discussion. Familiarize yourself with the rules and regulations of your institution and/or professional association. Ensure you have general and culturally specific resources about support services that you can share with students (these services may be on and off campus).

Take care of yourself. Be self-reflective. This not only models good practice to your students but it will also help you deal with your own emotional response. Get support for yourself and find out if your institution supports your teaching of sensitive topics. If it does not, there may be opportunity to find support through your professional networks or academic association.

It is to step three that this chapter now turns. How do we source appropriate materials and resources? The resources referenced in this book are a useful starting point, and provide a coherent and rigorously constructed set of curriculum materials and faculty guidelines for teaching about victimization which acknowledge that students may have their own experiences of crime.

Exercises to counter victim-blaming in the classroom

It would be impossible to document here a definitive range of case studies or set of materials that would cover every eventuality that might arise within a class on victimology. For some students, a class on victimology may present the first opportunity to articulate their own attitudes and beliefs. These first attempts are often difficult. Student discussions often teeter on the edge of awkward "political correctness" and other tensions surrounding clear expression. Consider the number of topics in victimology: they may include such things as portrayal of women in popular culture, cultures of masculinity, and murder rates of Black populations. It is not always easy to maintain a balance between free and clear expression of opinions and limiting offensive talk: some topics simply cannot be discussed without traversing these intersections. One approach in tackling this is to get students to write a paragraph about a specific issue in different styles. So one style could be as though two people were chatting over a coffee, another could be a newspaper article, another for a government report: you can be imaginative. Students can then compare and contrast the texts. This helps them to focus on what matters in victimology. What languages choices should they make? Which details are critical? How can they tell "good" from "bad" language? Are value judgments being made? With your years of experience this might seem obvious, but for students these details can only be assessed through practice.

As mentioned earlier, sometimes in the classroom questions emerge about a victim's behavior and responsibility. Almost any student can be tempted to blame the victim, particularly if the topic under discussion raises emotional responses, if there are conflicting explanations about events, or if the teacher introduces pressure to prematurely resolve dilemmas. Some students may be unfamiliar with the theoretical material and only know what they have previously seen and heard about in the media. It isn't easy to fit new information into one's existing world view. Talking about crime prevention and safe behavior is important in relation to rape and sexual violence and so too is the issue of responsibility. It is easy for students to lose sight of the basic principle of criminal responsibility and instead blame the victim. I have been using an exercise for around 15 years and it has been changed and adapted but its origin goes back to the 1970s (Borkenhagen, 1975). You will need two students who are not afraid to over-act for this role play exercise.

Exercise one – Mr. Smith and the robbery

This exercise uses humor to challenge the idea that the victim is to blame for crimes committed against her/him. It challenges students to think critically about who is the responsible party in relation to crime. Two students take the role of the police officer and Mr. Smith, reading aloud from the script which can be found in the *American Bar Association Journal* (Borkenhagen, 1975) and adapted and reproduced on numerous websites.

Upon completion of the exercise, students should see how ridiculous it is to blame someone for being robbed, even when there might be a prior history of the "victim" giving money away. This opens up the possibility of a debate about how we understand consent to sexual activity. This also unmasks some of the myths and stereotypes surrounding rape, providing a space for class discussion of why myths persist within modern culture and can sometimes result in placing the blame onto the victim. My students have a lot of fun with this exercise and there is usually a good deal of laughter during the reading of the script. For some they do not realize that it is a parody, using the reporting of a robbery as an analogy for rape, but they will "get it." Students have followed this exercise by searching media articles on rape cases to see if there are victim blaming narratives underpinning the reporting. A follow up to this exercise could also examine the percentage of women reporting rape to the police who go on to see the accused man sentenced in court. This would help to open up a discussion about how rape culture has an impact on the reporting and prosecution of such offences.

Exercise two – Sleeping with the Enemy

The second exercise requires viewing the film, *Sleeping with the Enemy* (1991), which highlights many aspects of domestic violence and victim-blaming behavior, and so might provoke strong responses from students. Preface engagement with this material with a caution to students that they may want to watch the video in short sections at their own pace. The suggested book, *Living with the Dominator* (Craven, 2008), was inspired by the Duluth Domestic Violence Intervention Project in Minnesota.

The aim of this exercise is to explore the issues of domestic violence and victim blaming. The video and accompanying book address myths surrounding domestic abuse which may lead to victim-blaming comments such as "why doesn't she leave?" and "I wouldn't put up with that." Students will find that there are examples in the video where they spot blaming behavior and this exercise allows them the space to see them in action and to articulate the impact of such behavior.

Summary

As an educator teaching victimology you will hear things that you find hard to believe. Indeed you will hear things you might not want to hear. In this respect the role of educator is not dissimilar to the role of researcher. As a researcher whose focus is sexual violence, Rebecca Campbell once wrote "My job is to listen to women's stories of rape" (2002, p.1) and she goes on to recount how the experiences of one rape survivor forever changed how she understood herself as a researcher. As an educator teaching victimology, you also will hear things you'll wish you could "un-hear" but the chances are that they will change you and how you teach. When you hear stories that are shocking, try not to show this on your face. One fleeting glance might be all it takes to close down the bravery that your student has summoned in approaching you. Victim blaming can be triggered by the most trivial of moments. So ensure that you model good behavior. Likewise if you feel that someone is not being truthful, try to avoid judging as they may be dealing with a truth that is too hard to share.

There are many other types of victim-blaming behavior that might occur in the classroom, but what this chapter has tried to provide are deeper understandings and practical responses. The tactic of engaging a whole class in an exercise means that the focus does not stay with the blaming comment. The classroom should be a space where students are challenged as well as given the opportunity to reflect. Having a range of exercises available which require few if any resources means that you can, at a moment's notice, engage the student in active learning which directly relates to the topic. Sometimes we need to seize the moment but we need strategies for doing so without entering into an argument or power play with a student.

Be mindful that you may not always succeed. As educators we can only open the door to reflection. As a wise woman once said to me "We can explain it to them but we cannot understand it for them." Only the student can do the hard work for themselves. Some students will resist, others will grasp the opportunity to challenge themselves. Often we can never guess in advance whose hearts and minds are ready to be opened; the delight of teaching is being there when it happens.

Appendix

Recommended resources

A National Scope Demonstration Project: Integrating Crime Victims Issues into University and College Curricula. Part of this project is to develop curriculum materials that faculty can use or adapt across a wide range of courses and disciplines. Materials are currently available for people to pilot in their classes at: http://www.uml.edu/FAHSS/Crim inal-Justice/victims-issues/victims-materials.aspx

Academy of Criminal Justice Sciences (http://www.acjs.org): This society provides online access to two official journals, *Justice Quarterly* and the *Journal of Criminal Justice Education*, as a membership benefit. The *Journal of Criminal Justice Education* contains a wealth of articles on the pedagogy of criminal justice education.

Freedom Programme: Based in the UK, this programme produces materials for working with issues of domestic abuse. Even the cartoons used to illustrate the website and the associated publications are useful teaching tools. See http://www.freedomprogramme.co.uk

Office for Victims of Crime: The OVC has a DVD entitled *Victim Impact: Listen and Learn* which includes a series of first-person accounts of crime victims and survivors. In each vignette, victims share their experiences and talk about the impact the victimization had on them and their families, friends and community. The videos and a facilitator manual are all available online: https://www.ovcttac.gov/VictimIm pact/presenters_toolbox.cfm

What Happens to the Brain During Sexual Assault: Watch a Seminar with Dr. Rebecca Campbell. In the latest Research for the Real World presentation, Campbell discusses the neurobiology of sexual assault and the effect trauma has on victim behavior. See: http://nij.gov/multi media/welcome.htm#presenter-campbell

Sleeping with the Enemy exercise

Steps

1. Assign students to read the book *Living with the Dominator* (http:// tinyurl.com/cfcujzh), which accompanies a victim assistance pro-gramme in the UK called The Freedom Programme. In the book the different personas of the Dominator are given names such as "The Bully" and "The King of the Castle."
2. Pre-video, ask students to select one of the "personas" from the book (The Bully, The King of the Castle, etc.) or you could assign different "personas" to your students, and ask them to imagine what sort of blaming behavior "he" might use. An example would be "The Bully" who uses intimidation and anger.
3. Require that students watch *Sleeping with the Enemy* in their own time making notes on when they spot the perpetrator using the traits of their chosen "persona" from the book. In the video, Julia

Roberts plays Laura, a young, married woman who apparently leads a happy life. But behind closed doors, her husband controls her every move.

4. In class students discuss who their chosen persona was and in which sections of the video they spotted him.

Acknowledgements

As a whole, this chapter is a reflection of practice, as experienced by a number of academics who teach victimology and I am particularly grateful to friends and colleagues in the United States and in the United Kingdom who have offered suggestions and contributions. The chapter would no doubt be different if we were philosophers or psychologists rather than criminologists but the hope is that it has resonance for all those who teach victimology. My thanks go to the many criminal justice educators and experts who assisted me in suggesting resources for this chapter, including the members of the American Society of Criminology, Division on Women and Crime. In particular I would like to thank Joanne Belknap, University of Colorado; Alison C. Cares, Assumption College; Ellen G. Cohn, Florida International University; Dana DeHart, University of South Carolina; Amy D'Unger, Georgia Institute of Technology; Tiff Jenson, Brigham Young University-Idaho; Kathrine Johnson, University of West Florida; Ráchael A. Powers, University of South Florida; Hannah Scott, University of Ontario Institute of Technology.

Bibliography

American College Health Association, 2013. *American College Health Association-National College Health Association: Reference group data report Fall 2012.* [online] Hanover, MD: American College Health Association. Available at: http: <http://www.acha-ncha.org/docs/ACHA-NCHA-II_ReferenceGroup_Data Report_Fall2012.pdf > [Accessed 4 June 2013].

Anastasio, P.A. and Costa, D.M., 2004. Twice hurt: How newspaper coverage may reduce empathy and engender blame for female victims of crime. *Sex Roles,* 51, pp.535–42.

Bain, K., 2004. *What the best college teachers do.* Cambridge, MA: Harvard University Press.

Bergmann, J. and Sams, A., 2012. Flip your classroom: *Reach every student in every class every day.* United States: International Society for Technology in Education.

Berrington, E. and Jones, H., 2002. Reality vs myth: Constructions of women's insecurity. *Feminist Media Studies*, 2(3), pp.307–23.

Borkenhagen, C.K., 1975. The legal bias against rape victims (The rape of Mr. Smith). *American Bar Association Journal*, 61(4), p.464.

Campbell, R., 2002. *Emotionally involved: The impact of researching rape*. New York: Routledge.

Carmody, D.C. and Washington, L.M., 2001. Rape myth acceptance among college women: The impact of race and prior victimization. *Journal of Interpersonal Violence*, 16, pp.424–36.

Cowan, G., 2000. Women's hostility toward women and rape and sexual harassment myths. *Violence Against Women*, 6(3), pp.238–46.

Craven, P., 2008. *Living with the dominator*. Great Britain: Freedom Publishing.

Currier, D.M. and Carlson, J.H., 2009. "Women and Violence" changes students' attitudes about violence. *Journal of Interpersonal Violence*, 24(10), pp.1735–54.

Dussich, J.P., 2006. Victimology–past, present and future, *RESOURCE MATERIAL SERIES No. 70*, 116. [online] Available at: <http://www.peacepalacelibrary.nl/ebooks/files/UNAFEI_no70.pdf#page=121> [Accessed 4 June 2013].

Eigenberg, H. and Garland, T., 2008. Victim blaming: Is it "your fault" if you are a victim of crime? In: L. Moriarty, ed. 2008. ed., *Controversies in victimology*. 2nd ed. Cincinnati: Anderson. Ch.2.

Finlay, L. and Gough, B., 2003. *Reflexivity: A practical guide for researchers in health and social sciences*. Oxford: Blackwell Publishing.

Fisher, B.M., 2001. *No angel in the classroom: Teaching through feminist discourse*. New York: Rowman, Littlefield.

Fox, K.A. and Cook, C.L., 2011. Is knowledge power? The effects of a victimology course on victim blaming. *Journal of Interpersonal Violence*, 26(17), pp.3407–27.

Freire, P., 1970. *Pedagogy of the oppressed*. New York: Seabury.

Hentig, von H., 1948. *The criminal and his victim*. New Haven: Yale University Press.

hooks, b., 1994. *Teaching to transgress: Education as the practice of freedom*. New York: Routledge.

——, 2003. *Teaching community. A pedagogy of hope*, New York: Routledge.

Jones, H. and Cook, K., 2008. *Rape crisis: Responding to sexual violence*. Dorset: Russell House.

Karmen, A., 1992. *Crime victims*. Pacific Grove: Brooks/Cole.

Larrivee, B., 2000. Transforming teaching practice: becoming the critically reflective teacher. *Reflective Practice*, 1(3), pp.293–307.

Loughran, J.J., 2006. *Developing a pedagogy of teacher education: Understanding teaching and learning about teaching*. London: Routledge.

Lowe, P. and Jones, H., 2010. Editorial. Enhanced learning in the social sciences, 2(3). [online]. Available at: <http://journals.heacademy.ac.uk/doi/full/10.11120/elss.2010.02030001> [Accessed 4 June 2013].

Malkin, C. and Stake, J.E., 2004. Changes in social attitudes and self-confidence in the women's and gender studies classroom: The role of teacher alliance and student cohesion. *Sex Roles*, 50, pp.455–68.

Mendelsohn, B., 1963. The origin of the doctrine of victimology. *Excerpta Criminologica*, 3(30): pp.239–44.

Nickoli, A.M., Hendricks, C., Hendricks, J.E. and Osgood, E., 2003. Pop culture, crime and pedagogy, *Journal of Criminal Justice Education*, 14 (1), pp.149–62.

Schon, D.A., 1983. *The reflective practitioner.* New York: Basic Books.

Shulman, L.S., 1986. Those who understand: Knowledge growth in teaching. Educational Researcher, 15(2), pp.4–14.

Sleeping with the Enemy. 1991. [DVD] *Sleeping with the Enemy.* California: Twentieth Century Fox Film Corporation.

Stampler, L., 2011. SlutWalks sweep the nation. *The Huffington Post,* [online] 20 April. Available at: <http://www.huffingtonpost.com/2011/04/20/slutwalk united-states-city_n_851725.html > [accessed 4 June 2013].

Truman, J.L. and Planty, M., 2011. *Criminal victimization bulletin.* [online] Bureau of Justice Statistics. Available at: <http://bjs.ojp.usdoj.gov/content/pub/pdf/cv11.pdf> [accessed 4 June 2013].

4

STILL AT THE PERIPHERY

Teaching race, ethnicity, crime, and justice

Helen Taylor Greene

The issue of race has a long history in the study of criminology and criminal justice (C/CJ) although the coverage of it often times was incomplete. According to Walker, et al. (2012, p.2), "Nearly every problem related to criminal justice issues involves matters of race and ethnicity." In the early 1900s some texts included chapters on race and crime but often omitted topics such as slave patrols and lynching (Gabbidon and Taylor Greene, 2013). Much later in the twentieth century, the neglect of race in criminal justice education received the attention of numerous scholars (see Young and Sulton, 1991; LaFree and Russell, 1993; Walker and Brown, 1995; Young and Taylor Greene, 1995). Today, many C/CJ programs include a race and crime course (with varying titles) in their curriculum. Race, ethnicity, crime, and justice books, edited volumes, journal articles and other resources are more readily available today than in the past (see, for example, Russell, et al., 2000; Gabbidon, et al., 2013).

In spite of more attention that is devoted to the study of race, ethnicity, crime, and justice, these courses continue to challenge both faculty and students. Consider the following questions:

Who should teach these courses when there is no race and crime scholar on the faculty?

Is it possible to teach a race and crime course without extensive knowledge of the subject matter?

Will teaching a race and crime course adversely impact one's teaching evaluations? (This is especially important to consider early in one's career)

Is it possible to deconstruct and reconstruct years of misinformation about race and crime in one course?

Answers to these questions will depend on many factors including (1) a professor's teaching experience, (2) the demographic characteristics of both professors and students, as well as (3) the racial climate of the department, institution and region of the country where the course is taught. Although challenging for some professors and students, these courses provide an opportunity to not only understand race and crime, but to appreciate its historical context and contemporary complexities. In this chapter the challenges of teaching race, ethnicity, crime and justice (RECJ)[1] courses are presented, then best practices and recommendations for success are identified. It begins with a brief overview of pedagogical issues in the study of race and crime.

Pedagogical reconstruction

Young and Taylor Greene (1995, p.88) used the term pedagogical reconstruction to refer to the need to integrate the historical and contemporary works on African Americans and crime into the C/CJ curriculum. The first group of "race scholars" who studied what is now referred to as the intersection of race, class, gender and crime included W. E. B. DuBois, Ida B. Wells Barnett, Monroe Work and E. Franklin Frazier. With the exception of Ida B. Wells Barnett, these early scholars completed their graduate work at predominantly white institutions (PWUs) including Harvard University (W. E. B. DuBois) and the University of Chicago (Monroe Work and E. Franklin Frazier) and later taught at Historically Black Colleges and Universities (HBCUs).

I became aware of these scholars when I was a doctoral student at the University of Maryland in the mid-1970s working with Dr. Julius

Debro on a funded research project to identify the contributions of black scholars to the study of criminology/criminal justice. Shortly thereafter I proposed a Blacks and Crime course to the department chair and was told the course would fit better in the African American Studies Department. This surprised me because the focus of the course was not just on African Americans but also on crime! Looking back, I often reflect on the fact that perhaps graduate students were not supposed to propose courses. It took fifteen more years before I was able to teach a course about Blacks, Crime and Justice.

The influx of African Americans and other minorities into the academy was a major impetus for recognition of the need for a more inclusive and historically accurate approach to the study of race and crime. This occurred in C/CJ graduate programs in the 1980s and 1990s. Gradually, more courses developed that are now known as race and crime courses.

Even though the theoretical and research contributions of race and crime scholars are recognized today, little is known about graduate level race and crime courses. We do know that there are more than 470 traditional and online master's C/CJ programs.[2] Since looking at all the graduate programs is beyond the scope of this chapter, an online analysis of courses offered at thirty-five C/CJ graduate programs that belong to the Association of Doctoral Programs in Criminology and Criminal Justice (ADPCCJ) found race and crime courses in only fourteen traditional and four online programs.[3] This indicates that it is important to continue pedagogical reconstruction at the graduate level since these courses often serve as the first step in preparing the next cadre of those who will teach race and crime courses in the academy and develop future race and crime scholars.

Challenges related to teaching race, ethnicity, crime, and justice

Regardless of the subject matter of a course, the professor is a key to its success or failure. They must be knowledgeable, enthusiastic and capable of maintaining student interest in the subject matter. Assuming that professors assigned to teach RECJ courses possess these qualities, why is teaching RECJ often more challenging than teaching more traditional courses? That is, these courses not only require in-depth knowledge of the subject matter that may vary depending on the course title, but the likelihood of student resistance is higher due to the topic matter and their unwillingness to take these courses. This may be viewed as anecdotal but I challenge any person reading this to start a discussion about race and ethnicity with anyone and watch their reaction.

As Mann (1993, p.3) so aptly stated, "Definitions can be problematic, especially when the topic is race or ethnicity." Mann proposed that "minorities" is the best term for describing race or ethnicity. However, that term excludes whites who are also included in race and crime courses. In this chapter race refers to both an individual's physical characteristics and how these characteristics are socially constructed. Ethnicity refers to a group that might share physically identifiable traits as well as a language, culture and place of origin (Gabbidon and Taylor Greene, 2013). In spite of limitations, here we use the U.S. Census Bureau's racial/ethnic categories: Native Americans, Whites, African Americans, Hispanic/Latino Americans and Asian Americans. Current definitions of race and ethnicity are less than desirable as the following examples demonstrate:

Is the child of Nigerian parents born in the United States an African American? Nigerian American?
Is the child of bi-cultural parents (for example who are American and Jamaican) African American or Jamaican American? Depending on their skin color their race could be perceived as Black or other.
Does a dark skin American whose parents were born in the Dominican Republic belong to the category of Black American or the Latina/o ethnic category?
Is the child of colored South African parents born in the United States a Black American?
How are interracial/mixed race Americans categorized?

The best way to explain these definitional challenges is to point out that there is considerable diversity within racial and ethnic groups (including whites) and that culture, color/hue, nation of origin, class and region matter as well (Georges-Abeyie, 1989 cited in Gabbidon, Taylor Greene and Young, 2002). Relatedly, "Biological differences between individuals especially color and hue, provide the foundation for what many refer to as the social construction of race" (Aguirre and Turner, 2011 cited in Taylor Greene, 2011, p.96). Getting students to understand how race is a social construction is a challenging task.

The challenge of faculty preparation

Many faculty members who teach these courses are not prepared to do so. As demonstrated above regarding the lack of graduate level race courses, most are likely novices, unfamiliar with the race and crime body of knowledge and scholars. If you ask your colleagues (and your students) to identify five African American, Latina/Latino American, Native American and Asian American scholars, will they succeed? Can they identify five publications by minority scholars? Do they know the leading historical and contemporary white race and crime scholars? Second, few criminologists either choose race and crime as an area of specialization, or have the opportunity to work with race and crime scholars during graduate school. As a result, some faculty members may find themselves teaching a RECJ course that they themselves know very little about. This is especially true for junior faculty in tenure track lines. Very often they are assigned to teach a RECJ course if there is not anyone else. Not only are some junior faculty challenged by the subject matter, their inexperience as professors present another challenge that will likely effect their student evaluations.

Several other factors contribute to the lack of preparation of faculty to teach RECJ including (1) the "status" of race and crime in C/CJ graduate programs, (2) its historical existence on the periphery as opposed to a focus on the core of the body of knowledge and (3) ongoing trepidation/anxiety about race and crime amongst criminologists.

Even though the number of white and minority scholars that study race and crime in the contemporary era has increased, there is still trepidation/anxiety about race and racism amongst criminologists. This is due at least in part to the conundrum of minorities in the criminal justice system. Are Blacks, Latina/os and Native Americans more criminal? Is the criminal justice system racist? The answer to both questions are no, but past and present controversies surrounding racism in American society and criminal and juvenile justice are ongoing challenges. Finally, how do we prepare faculty to master the subject matter when it makes them uncomfortable and creates anxiety? At some point many faculty, especially those who have been "stuck in a race and crime course" will just want it to be over! Mastering these challenges has long term implications for both faculty and students.

The challenge of student resistance

As far as I know, there is very little research on student resistance in criminal justice courses. More than likely student resistance varies from one course, major and/or department to another. Some student resistance to course subject matter, course requirements and grading is to be expected. Student resistance is influenced by varying factors including but not limited to instructor preparedness, course content and student readiness (Virginia Commonwealth University, n.d.; Zuniga and Mildred, 2005). When a student enters a race and crime course they usually bring with them ideas that are shaped by their experiences, attitudes, values and beliefs. Regardless of the subject matter, student resistance may vary depending on who is teaching the course (Moore, 1997) and the subject (Zuniga and Mildred, 2005). Although anecdotal, one black female who teaches a race and crime course disclosed to me that "My issue is a bit more complicated because I have a lot of white students who think I am a racist." Race is still an issue in our society and because of her skin color students may stereotype her before she even broaches the subject. This often places instructors of color at a disadvantage. However, a knowledgeable, enthusiastic and seasoned race and crime scholar who encounters student resistance stands a better chance of overcoming resistance based upon their familiarity with the subject matter and prior experience teaching the course.

For many students, regardless of their race, ethnicity, gender or age, studying race and crime might be as uncomfortable as it is for some faculty members to teach. In RECJ courses, students are required to learn/re-learn facts and figures that challenge their misperceptions about race and crime. Coverage of the historical material seems to be especially difficult for students. This is due, at least in part, to the inadequate coverage of historical information about race in America in other C/CJ courses and texts. Students I taught often expressed that "they weren't around back then" or "they aren't responsible for what happened in the past" and "we don't have those race problems anymore." Similarly, in conversation with a professor teaching at an HBCU, it was shared with me that some students have no clue about slavery and its continued impact on minorities. For some students (and faculty) the reality of the historical treatment of all race/ethnic groups, including white immigrants in our country is overwhelming. After students get past the historical material, the crime and victimization data is also problematic.

When I taught a course entitled Blacks, Crime and Justice the lecture on race, crime and victimization was one of my favorites! I pointed out that the majority of the US population is white and therefore the majority of persons arrested also are white; that regardless of race/ethnicity, most adults and juveniles are arrested for property not violent crimes, and that most persons arrested for drug abuse violations are white as well (FBI, 2013). Both majority and minority students were usually in disbelief. Graduate students are usually familiar with crime and victimization statistics and the disproportionality issue. In a graduate race and crime course, students will receive a much more comprehensive and uncomfortable discussion of crime and victimization that includes coverage of lynching and hate crime statistics.

Student resistance can be quite subtle and manifest in varying ways including silence, absences, underperformance, frustration and verbal challenges. It will also vary from one university to another. For example, student resistance in race and crime courses might be more pronounced at PWUs than at HBCUs, and in universities/colleges where there is a low minority population. Jones (2013) notes that students who come from privileged backgrounds often have not been exposed to some of the themes and topics covered in a typical race and crime class. If they have been exposed, it is often difficult for them to fully understand and/or appreciate those issues. African American students at a PWI were reluctant to express their perspectives "because of fear of ruining school spirit on campus" (Harrell, 2013). Relatedly, the racial climate of the university could impact student resistance in race and crime courses. Students might feel emboldened at a university that has less tolerance for diversity and affirmative action.

In spite of challenges, race and crime courses present an excellent opportunity to increase understanding of controversial topics amongst faculty and students. They also offer an opportunity for growth and can ignite interest in numerous topics, even amongst the most challenged and resistant individuals. To this end, the next section presents strategies for successfully teaching race and crime courses.

Suggested best practices for faculty teaching race and crime courses

If you have been assigned to teach a race and crime course for the first time – embrace it! If you have taught a race and crime course in the past – embrace it again and continue to improve! First and foremost, faculty should make a concerted effort to teach effectively. Those assigned to teach race and crime courses should begin with a self-assessment that includes a knowledge assessment, a willingness to adopt some of the suggested best practices and a commitment to continuing their education about historical and contemporary race and crime issues.

Self-assessment

The first step to successful teaching is an assessment of one's teaching philosophy, teaching style, attitudes and perspectives about race and crime, and knowledge of the race and crime body of knowledge. Consider the following:

Is your teaching philosophy and style student-centered? What is your own social location?
What is your perspective about race and crime?
Do you have any personal crime/victimization experiences that impact your perspective?

According to the University of Minnesota, Center for Teaching and Learning (2013, n.p.), a teaching philosophy is "a self-reflective statement of your beliefs about teaching and learning ... how you put your beliefs into practice ... what you do or anticipate doing in the classroom." One's teaching philosophy is related to their teaching style. Usually one's teaching style can be either instructor-centered or student-centered (Penn State, 2013). Instructor-centered approaches empower the professor while student-centered approaches empower students, often with the professor's guidance. Teaching race and crime courses will require both instructor and student-centered approaches, depending on the material being taught.

Faculty teaching race and crime courses will need to know their personal views about race and crime issues. Unnever and Gabbidon (2011) describe the unique worldview of African Americans that differs from that of whites and other minorities. This is applicable to others as well. Understanding one's worldview is the first step to recognizing and addressing any possible biases the faculty member might bring to teaching the course.

Knowledge assessment

After a self-assessment faculty should assess their knowledge of race and crime theories, research, books, journal articles and resources. Consider the following questions:

How many race and crime courses have you taken?
How many race and crime courses have you taught?
How many race and crime textbooks have you read?
How many race and crime journal articles have you recently read?
Who are the most important early race and crime scholars?
Who are the most important contemporary race and crime scholars?
What are the most important race and crime issues today?

Answers to these questions will determine how one should prepare for teaching a race and crime course. The suggested best practices presented next are aimed at improving preparation for teaching and guiding faculty towards developing an ongoing interest in the study of race and crime.

Even if you have not taught a race and crime course you can use your area of expertise and experience to better understand race and crime issues. For example, if your area of specialization or dissertation topic is related to corrections you probably already have been introduced to several contemporary race and crime topics such as mass incarceration, life sentences, wrongful convictions and collateral consequences. You may already be familiar with readings to include in this unit.

Preparation

Let's imagine that you are teaching a race and crime course for the first time, had one race and crime course in graduate school, read about two textbooks, ten journal articles and are familiar with a few historical and contemporary scholars. How will you prepare to teach the course? After panic subsides, step one should be to start preparing your lectures as soon as possible. This will include not only developing the syllabus but reading all the materials you will use in the course. The most logical next step is to choose at least one textbook with instructor resources that includes a student study site! Publishers have taken some of the anxiety out of preparing to teach many courses, even race and crime courses. The study site for the last edition of *Race and Crime* (Gabbidon and Taylor Greene, 2013), includes selected journal articles and several video clips. *The Color of Justice* (Walker, et al., 2012) has several student supplements including MindTap, a cloud-based platform with student learning tools. Text book selection is guided by the title of the course although either one or both of these two books should be required in a graduate course. Step three is to identify the course material that you will teach using either an instructor versus student-centered approach. Step four is to take the time to identify and develop the lectures that require more of your time.

The assessment of students enrolled in the course also is important during preparation. Teaching majority white versus black students might require different strategies. When the majority of students are either African Americans, Asian Americans, Latina/o Americans, Native Americans or Caucasian, course materials should include topics of interest to them. It is also important to make sure that these students do not feel marginalized in the classroom. That is sometimes certain voices are silenced due to the social makeup of the classroom. However, I am not suggesting calling out a certain person to speak on behalf of an entire group of people. I cannot stress enough how damaging it is, to call out a student to speak on behalf of their race, gender, sexuality or otherwise. A list of selected course readings should also be made available (see appendix for recommendations).

Continuing education

One should have a goal of increasing their familiarity and comfort level with teaching race and crime. This can be done with a commitment to race and crime continuing education. The most important issue for new, current and seasoned faculty teaching race and crime courses is to continue to stay abreast of recent theoretical and research developments. There are several traditional and more technological ways to do this including reading the recent journal literature, viewing race and crime programs, volunteering to write book reviews, signing up for journal alerts, participating in Webinars and identifying continuing education/faculty development opportunities.

Anyone that has attended either a regional or national professional criminology or criminal justice conference can attest to the numerous opportunities each provides for professional development, networking and time spent discussing teaching challenges with colleagues. Attending panel presentations by race and crime scholars and on race and crime topics will increase your understanding and permit you to network with these individuals. Use the book exhibit area to peruse recent race and crime publications and build your personal collection at a special conference attendee rate. Finally, faculty should consider presenting a paper on a race and crime topic of interest at one of the conferences. The paper can become a manuscript for submission as well as incorporated into teaching the course.

Reducing student resistance

My own experiences teaching race and crime have met with very little student resistance which I attribute to my experience, knowledge and enthusiasm. There was more resistance to the subject matter among white students at a PWU than amongst Black students at HBCUs. That said, one of the best race and crime courses I taught was at the PWU. Student enthusiasm and interest was very high and student resistance during the course was practically nonexistent.[4] Included here are several strategies to reduce student resistance that work for me along with suggestions from junior scholars that teach the course at PWUs. These best practices include:

Establish ground rules for collegiality and respect in the course
Utilize knowledge assessments of subject matter to guide lecture presentations throughout the course
Include assignments on the background of race and crime scholars included in the course
Require research projects
Utilize teaching aids that enhance course material

During the introductory lecture for RECJ courses the importance of collegiality and respect for the opinions of others should be addressed. According to Harris (2013, n.p.),

> One of the most important challenges … is to allow students a forum where each is able to voice their opinions … I require each student to agree via a verbal contract that they will respect each other's POV (point of view). I spend 30 minutes of the initial class giving students time to stand up, shake hands and cement the verbal class contract.

Making it clear that it is important to respect the opinions of others will dissipate very loud and disorderly exchanges when presenting and discussing controversial topics. Allowing students an opportunity to network with others taking the course begins to break down barriers that might exist between those of different racial and ethnic backgrounds.

Regardless of student demographics, assessments of knowledge both at the beginning of and throughout the course are helpful. A lecture on the history of race and crime in America could begin by asking each student to respond to a series of questions about the experiences of varying racial/ethnic groups. The lecture on the extent of crime and victimization could assess students' knowledge of the representation of whites and minorities in arrest and victimization data. The number of knowledge assessments will vary and are not necessary for every topic covered in the course.

Familiarizing students with contemporary race and crime scholars is another helpful strategy. This can be done by encouraging students to include background information about authors in course assignments. I do this for oral journal article critiques and term project presentations.[5] Online access to biographical information is readily available and students can contact contemporary scholars by email and other social media. Scholars and textbook authors can be invited to participate in a course lecture via Skype and videoconferencing.

Student-centered research projects allow students to empirically validate issues of race and crime on their own (Jones, 2013). Utilizing a "delegator" teaching style the professor is a consultant who acts as a guide and puts the responsibility and control for learning on students (Penn State, 2013). The role of the professor is to introduce topics like differential involvement and differential treatment, and then guide students through the development and implementation of a research project "to help them understand, through empirical data, the reality of issues pertaining to race and crime" (Jones, 2013).

Conclusion

The purpose of this chapter was to identify challenges and best practices for teaching graduate race and crime courses. It began with a brief overview of the history of the study of race and crime and its integration into the study of C/CJ. As previously stated, graduate race and crime courses are important for several reasons including their role in preparing faculty who will teach these courses and race and crime scholars. As a matter of fact, I prefer the integrated approach that includes race and crime content in every course. This has been my approach for several years. I believe the best way to successfully teach race and crime courses is to embrace the challenges they present and utilize strategies that work best for you. These courses provide an excellent opportunity to contribute to the body of knowledge as well because there are many areas that remain unexplored. For example what factors, if any, contribute to effective preparation for teaching race and crime in graduate programs? More analyses of course content and race and crime textbooks is necessary. Most importantly I believe it is important to do what is required to get it right!

Appendix

Recommended reading list

Alexander, M., 2011. *The new Jim Crow: Mass incarceration in the age of colorblindness*. New York: The New Press.

Barak, G., Leighton, P. and Flavin, J., 2010. *Class, race, gender and crime*. 3rd ed. Lanham, Maryland: Rowman and Littlefield.

Chavez-Garcia, M., 2012. *States of delinquency: Race and science in the making of California's juvenile justice system*. Berkeley and Los Angeles, CA: University of California.

Cochran, J.C. and Warren, P.Y., 2012. Racial, ethnic, and gender differences in perceptions of the police: The salience of officer race within the context of racial profiling. *Journal of Contemporary Criminal Justice*, 28, pp.206–27.

Eitle, T., Eitle, D. and Johnson-Jennings, M., 2013. General strain theory and substance use among American Indian adolescents. *Race and Justice*, 3, pp.3–30.

Feld, B.C., 1999. *Bad kids: Race and the transformation of the juvenile court*. New York: Oxford University Press.

Free, M.D., Jr. and Ruesnik, M., 2012. *Race and justice: Wrongful convictions of African American men*. Boulder, CO: Lynne Reiner Publishers.

Gabbidon. S.L., 2007. *Criminological perspectives on race and crime*. New York: Routledge.

Gabbidon, S.L., 2010. *Race, ethnicity, crime, and justice*. Thousand Oaks, CA: Sage.

Gabbidon, S.L., Higgins, G. and Nelson, M., 2012. Public support for racial profiling in airports: Results from a statewide poll. *Criminal Justice Policy Review*, 23, pp.254–69.

Georges-Abeyie, D., 1989. Race, ethnicity, and the spatial dynamic: Toward a realistic study of black crime, crime victimization, and criminal justice processing of blacks. In: S. Gabbidon, H. Taylor Greene and V. Young, eds. 2002. *African American classics in criminology and criminal justice*. Thousand Oaks, CA: Sage. Ch.16

Hawkins, D., 2011. Things fall apart: Revisiting race and ethnic differences in criminal violence amidst a crime drop. *Race and Justice*, 1, pp.3–48.

Jones, N., 2010. *Between good and ghetto*. Piscataway, NJ: Rutgers University Press.

Kalunta-Crumpton, A. ed., 2012. *Race, ethnicity, crime and criminal justice in the Americas*. Basingstoke, United Kingdom: Palgrave Macmillan.

Kennedy, R., 1997. *Race, crime and the law*. New York: Pantheon Books.

Krimsky, S. and Sloan K. eds., 2011. *Race and the genetic revolution: Science, myth, and culture*. New York: Columbia University.

Miller, J., 2009. *Getting played*. New York: New York University Press.

Muhammed, K., 2011. *The condemnation of blackness*. Cambridge, MA: Harvard University Press.

Potter, H., 2008. *Battle cries: Black women and intimate partner abuse*. New York: New York University Press.

Rios, V., 2011. *Punished: Policing the lives of black and Latino boys*. New York: New York University Press.

Ross, L., 1998. *African American criminologists, 1970–1996: An annotated bibliography*. Westport, CT: Greenwood.

Russell, K., 1998. *The color of crime: Racial hoaxes, White fear, black protectionism, police harassment and other macroaggressions*. New York: New York University Press.

Russell, K., 2004. *Underground codes: Race, crime, and related fires*. New York: New York University Press.

Taylor Greene, H. and Gabbidon, S.L., 2000. *African-American criminological thought*. Albany, NY: State University of New York Press.

Taylor Greene, H. and Gabbidon, S.L., 2009. *The encyclopedia of race and crime*. Thousand Oaks, CA: Sage.

Unnever, J.D. and Cullen, F.T, 2011. White perceptions of whether African Americans and Hispanics are prone to violence and support for the death penalty. *Journal of Research in Crime and Delinquency*, 49(4), pp.519–44.

Ward, G., 2012. *The black child savers*. Chicago, IL: University of Chicago.

Withrow, B.L. and Dailey, J.D., 2012. Racial profiling litigation: Current status and emerging controversies. *Journal of Contemporary Criminal Justice*, 28, pp.122–45.

Young, V. and Reviere, R., 2006. *Women behind bars*. Boulder, CO: Lynne Rienner Publishers.

Recommended websites

http://www.tandfonline.com/action/showMostReadArticles?journalCod
e=wecj20#.UtcZFvvvJ3U (Most read journal articles from *Journal of
Ethnicity in Criminal Justice*)

http://raj.sagepub.com/reports/most-read (Most read journal articles
from *Race and Justice*)

www.deathpenaltyinfo.org

http://www.sentencingproject.org

Notes

1 In this chapter "race, ethnicity, crime and justice" and "race and crime" are
used interchangeably.
2 This information comes from my search for C/CJ programs on
GradSchools.com.
3 This information comes from my analysis of members of the Association of
Doctoral Programs in Criminology and Criminal Justice with graduate race
and crime courses. The list of members is available in Appendix B, p.36 at:
http://www.adpccj.com/documents/2013survey.pdf.
4 This was an undergraduate course.
5 I do this in other courses as well.

Bibliography

Aguirre, Jr. A. and Turner, J. H., 2011. American ethnicity: The dynamics and
consequences of discrimination. 7th ed. New York: McGraw-Hill Higher
Education.

Federal Bureau of Investigation, 2013. *Crime in the United States 2012 Table
43A*. [online] Available at: <http://www.fbi.gov/about-us/cjis/ucr/crime-
in-the-u.s/2012/crime-in-the-u.s.-2012/tables/43tabledatadecoverviewpdf>
[Accessed 13 January 2014].

Gabbidon, S.L. and Taylor Greene, H., 2013. *Race and crime*. 3rd ed. Thousand
Oaks, CA: Sage.

Gabbidon, S.L., Taylor Greene, H. and Young, V.D., 2002. *African American
classics in criminology and criminal justice*. Thousand Oaks, CA: Sage.

Georges-Abeyie, D., 1989. Race, ethnicity, and the spatial dynamic. *Social
Justice*, 16, pp.35–54.

Harrell, D., 2013. 'Email correspondence to greeneht@tsu.edu'. Sent Monday
16 December 2013: 03:11pm.

Harris, J., 2013. 'Email correspondence to greeneht@tsu.edu'. Sent Tuesday
17 December 2013: 12:34pm.

Jones, C., 2013. 'Email correspondence to greeneht@tsu.edu'. Sent Thursday
19 December 2013: 07:59am.

LaFree, G. and Russell, K.K., 1993. Special issue: The peripheral core of criminal justice education the argument for studying race and crime. *Journal of Criminal Justice Education*, 4(2), pp.273–98.

Mann, C.R., 1993. *Unequal justice: A question of color.* Bloomington, IN: Indiana University Press.

Moore, M., 1997. Student resistance to course content: Reactions to the gender of the messenger. *Teaching Sociology*, 25, pp.128–33.

Penn State Learning Design Community Hub University, 2013. *Teaching styles.* [online] Available at: <http://ets.psu.edulearningdesign/audience/teaching styles> [Accessed on 19 December 2013].

Russell, K.K., Jones, J. and Pfeifer, H., 2000. *Race and crime: An annotated bibliography.* Westport, CJ: Greenwood Press.

Taylor Greene, H., 2011. Race and crime. In M. Maguire and D. Okada, eds. *Critical issues in crime and justice.* Thousand Oak, CA: Sage. Ch.7

University of Minnesota Center for Teaching and Learning, 2013. *Writing your teaching philosophy.* [online] Available at: <http://www1.umn.edu/ohr/tea chlearn/tutorials/philosophy/> [Accessed 19 December 2013].

Unnever, J.D. and Gabbidon, S.L., 2011. *A theory of African American offending: Race, racism, and crime.* New York: Routledge.

Virginia Commonwealth University, n.d. *Center for Teaching Excellence.* [online] Available at: <http://www.vcu.edu/cte/resources> [Accessed 7 January 2014].

Walker, S. and Brown, M., 1995. A pale reflection of reality: The neglect of racial and ethnic minorities in introductory criminal justice textbooks. *Journal of Criminal Justice Education*, 6(1), pp.61–84.

Walker, S., Spohn, C. and DeLone, M., 2012. *The color of justice: Race, ethnicity, and crime in America.* 5th ed. Belmont, CA: Thomson Wadsworth.

Young, V.D. and Sulton, A.T., 1991. Excluded: The current status of African American scholars in the field of criminology and criminal justice. *Journal of Research in Crime and Delinquency*, 28, pp.108–16.

Young, V.D. and Taylor Greene, H., 1995. Pedagogical reconstruction: Incorporating African-American perspectives into the curriculum. *Journal of Criminal Justice Education*, 6(1), pp.85–104.

Zuniga, Z. and Mildred, J., 2005. Resistance in the diverse classroom: Meanings and opportunities. *On Campus with Women*, 34(1–2). Available through: http://www.aacu.org/ocww/volume34_1/feature.cfm?section=1 [Accessed 7 January 2014].

5

THE INVISIBLE MINORITY

Making the LGBT community visible in the criminal justice classroom

Emily Lenning

> In many ways, they are an invisible minority. They are arrested, beaten, terrorized, even executed. Many are treated with contempt and violence by their fellow citizens while authorities empowered to protect them look the other way or, too often, even join in the abuse. They are denied opportunities to work and learn, driven from their homes and countries, and forced to suppress or deny who they are to protect themselves from harm.
>
> Hillary Clinton, Secretary of State, 2011

Secretary of State Hillary Clinton, in her groundbreaking Human Rights Day speech, made history by dedicating her entire address to the experiences of lesbian, gay, bisexual, and transgender (LGBT) citizens around the globe. For those of us who identify as LGBT, it was perhaps one of the most powerful and validating speeches to ever cross the lips of a U.S. politician. The way Clinton succinctly described the discrimination and violence that I, as a lesbian, face – and yet at the same time labeling me as an "invisible minority" (thus, presumably protected and hidden) – truly captured the way I have felt my whole life. I am sure I am not the only LGBT person who has felt simultaneously vulnerable, threatened, and completely invisible. While the LGBT community does face some of the same problems as "visible" minorities (e.g., racial minorities) our life experiences are somewhat complicated by the fact that, for the most part, our minority status is only made visible to others when we choose to. This does not mean that we do not experience the same forms of discrimination and violence as other minorities, but that we often suffer in silence without that suffering being recognized by others. It is, quite literally, as if it only exists *to us*. The invisible nature of our sexual and/or gender orientation pushes us even further from public attention, which is perhaps why still, even today, Secretary Clinton's speech was necessary decades after other minorities have been given legal protections. Unfortunately, institutions of higher learning and the disciplines within them are but microcosms of society, which means that the LGBT community continues to be invisible or, at most, an afterthought in nearly all curricula, including that of criminal justice (Cannon and Dirks-Linhorst, 2006).

Criminal justice education, in general, must be applauded for its continued and growing recognition that minorities have unique and revealing experiences within our criminal justice system. Largely, however, our inclusion of minorities in criminal justice curricula has been limited to addressing "visible" minorities (Fradella, et al., 2009). Indeed, when we teach about "visible" minorities in criminal justice, we have come to implicitly recognize that there are multiple dimensions to their experiences that must be considered in the classroom. Though it has not always been this way, the inclusion of race, class, and gender in the curriculum has become common in criminal justice departments across the country.

Considering issues of race, class, and gender in the classroom we have reached a point where the majority of criminal justice professors understand that these issues must be addressed in everything we teach. Take racial minorities, for example – most criminal justice courses consider race in relation to nearly everything. When we discuss policing, we not only discuss multi-racial police/citizen interaction, but the issue of diversity among officers as well. When we teach about incarceration, we inevitably show our students charts and graphs that illustrate the racial inequality in incarceration and, more importantly, discuss the social and political context within which disparity occurs. The same is true of sentencing, victimology, and a variety of other sub-topics within criminal justice.

When it comes to the "invisible" minority, though, many of us struggle to see that there are multiple dimensions to their experiences as well. In my experience, criminal justice professors – especially, but not exclusively, heterosexual professors – fail to take discussions about LGBT issues in criminal justice beyond a superficial discussion of discrimination or violence against them. I would venture to guess that for many of us, if we were asked to teach about LGBT issues (which, unfortunately, we are not often asked to do), our initial "go-to" topic would be hate crimes. The most sympathetic of us may pull some data from the UCR hate crime statistics and we may even go so far as to talk about Matthew Shepard or show the popular film *Boys Don't Cry*, about the murder of transgender teen Brandon Teena. While hate crimes are an important issue, and putting faces to this violence may sensitize our students to the consequences of homophobia, to limit our discussions about the LGBT community to hate crimes does our students a great disservice.

Just as Bonilla-Silva (2006) made the argument about color-blindness allowing white people to deny racial inequality, "sexuality-blindness" likewise allows heterosexuals to deny sexual inequality. We must not ignore that there are multiple and consequential issues facing LGBT individuals in criminal justice and the field of criminal justice education. A comprehensive criminal justice curriculum must include a consideration of sexuality not only as it relates to violence against sexual and gender minorities, but as it relates to people's experiences within the institutions of criminal justice as offenders, victims, professionals, and scholars. To not do so is sending our students the message that their interactions with the LGBT community – no matter how they play out – are innocuous and require no forethought. While unfortunately some of our students may have to deal with extreme violence against sexual minorities in their future capacity as CJ professionals, the truth is that they will come into everyday contact with the LGBT community far more often. Therefore, it is essential that they do so in a respectful, empathetic, and informed manner. This, of course, means that we need to teach them how to do that. The only way to do that is to make the LGBT community completely visible in everything we teach, and hopefully the tips that follow will make that an easier task.

Lifting the veil: putting the invisible in plain sight

Due to the "invisible" nature of the LGBT community, chances are some of your students will not even realize that they have interacted with sexual minorities throughout their lives. As we all know, empathy is best learned through interaction with others and, if students have not knowingly or significantly interacted with sexual minorities and learned about their experiences, the first thing we need to do is make the LGBT experience visible. In most cases, this must begin with a basic lesson in terminology.

LGBTQIA ... what?

Do not make the mistake of assuming that your students (or even you) fully understand the above alphabet soup. Depending on how detailed your inclusion of sexual minorities in your class will be, you may want to start simple (e.g., LGBT) or address the whole gamut of possibilities and also define Queer,[1] Intersex,[2] and Ally.[3] In addition to providing basic definitions of these terms, you should plan on "unpacking" them – a thorough explanation of transgender, for example, requires an introductory discussion on the difference between biological sex and socially constructed gender roles. Once you are confident that students can grasp the symbolic nature of gender you can introduce the various dimensions of gender (i.e., presentation and orientation – see Lenning (2009) for a deeper explanation) and finally, describe the myriad of identities that fall under the umbrella of the term transgender. Within this context, it is imperative to point out to students that sexuality, biological sex, and gender identity are three distinct concepts and experiences and should never be conflated or thought to be inextricably linked to one another. If you have the sense that all of this, though basic and introductory, will be too complicated as a starting point for teaching about LGBT issues you can begin on a more basic level and couch these concepts within a broader discussion about culture and norms (which can then easily transition you into a discussion about gender norms, followed by sexual norms). Regardless of the order or degree to which you introduce these concepts, they should all be provided with the greater goal of revealing heterosexual privilege.

Revealing heterosexual privilege

The invisible nature of the LGBT experience makes exposing heterosexual privilege (and the hegemonic masculinity behind it) somewhat more difficult than revealing other forms of privilege (e.g., white privilege). However it is essential as a backdrop for introducing LGBT issues specific to the criminal justice system. After laying the definitional foundation outlined above, I introduce the concept of heterosexual privilege with a guided imagery exercise (provided in the appendix) in an effort to put my students into the shoes, so to speak, of an LGBT person. I have found that the most effective way to give students a visceral experience is not to ask them to imagine what it is like to be LGBT (as sexuality and gender are so engrained that this is nearly impossible), but to imagine what it is like to be heterosexual (which most students are quite familiar with) in a world where heterosexuality is *not* the norm. Either with their eyes closed or accompanied by a timed presentation of images,[4] I take students on a journey from childhood to college in the shoes of someone whose sexuality is different from the majority of the people around them. They experience the fear, shame, and alienation that are felt, unfortunately, by far too many LGBT individuals. Since heterosexual privileges are so engrained in every aspect of our culture, very few heterosexuals ever imagine what it would be like if the majority of the teachers they learn from, doctors they respect, friends they love, or celebrities they idolize were gay. Additionally, it is not a common experience for heterosexuals to lament over when to come out to the people around them, so to even think about being in such a predicament tends to be a huge eye-opener for students.

When we require students to see the world from a radically different vantage point they begin to understand not only the formal and informal freedoms that constitute heterosexual privilege, but exactly how it feels to not benefit from them. Doing the guided imagery prior to giving concrete examples of heterosexual privilege means that students will be more apt to appreciate that not being afforded these privileges can have extreme social, political, economic, and psychological consequences.

The concept of heterosexual privilege (also referred to as heteronormativity or compulsory heterosexuality) is most widely attributed to queer and/or feminist gender scholars (e.g., Rich, 1980; Rubin, 1984) and is in many respects akin to the more commonly recognized concept of "white privilege," whereby whites enjoy certain privileges for no other reason than the color of their skin. Though white privilege has been theorized and exposed for centuries, it was Peggy McIntosh (1989) who provided educators with arguably the most "user-friendly" classroom tool for describing white privilege in her classic essay "White privilege: Unpacking the invisible knapsack." Countless teachers and professors have used her examples (e.g., "I am never asked to speak for all the people of my racial group," "If a traffic cop pulls me over, or if the IRS audits my tax return, I can be sure I haven't been singled out because of my race") to demonstrate these unearned advantages. In recent years a similar list, this time providing examples of heterosexual privilege, has surfaced (Author Unknown)[5] and can be easily found on the Internet. This list serves as an extremely useful teaching tool. Most of the examples on the list, like the white privilege list, are informal examples of privilege (e.g., "I don't have to defend my heterosexuality," "People don't ask why I made my choice of sexual orientation") but the truth is that white privilege and heterosexual privileges have over time become more divergent. While both visible and invisible minorities face similar social stigma and informal discrimination, laws regarding visible minorities (racial minorities in particular) have made institutionalized stigma and institutionally sanctioned discrimination not impossible, but at least litigable.

As Clinton pointed out, invisible minorities continue to live in a world where they are purposely and legally denied the same civil rights that have served to humanize others and make informal discrimination against them significantly more egregious in our culture. While visible minorities have slowly but surely been afforded equal rights under the law, invisible minorities face legally sanctioned prejudice in every single social institution, including marriage, employment, housing, school, and healthcare.

Currently less than half of states in the U.S. allow gay marriage,[6] civil unions, or domestic partnerships and thirty-three states have laws or constitutional amendments that ban gay marriage altogether. Twenty-nine states have no laws protecting LGB[7] employees from discrimination in the workplace. The same number of states do not have any laws to protect LGBT individuals from being denied housing on the basis of their sexual or gender orientation. Eighteen states do not include LGBT youth in school anti-discrimination laws or anti-bullying laws. When it comes to healthcare, eighteen states consider same-sex couples to be legal strangers, which means they are denied the opportunity to make healthcare decisions on behalf of their partners (regardless of their wishes) and thirty-seven states do not include LGB partners in their FMLA policies. As you will find in the appendix, there are several organizations that provide easy-to-use interactive maps and other resources that you can use to demonstrate formalized compulsory heterosexuality to your students (including the *Movement Advancement Project*, from which the aforementioned information came). Describing these conditions to our students first and foremost brings to light the everyday lived experiences of people they otherwise may not even see (figuratively or literally), but also sets the stage for highlighting LGBT issues in the social institution of greatest concern to this book: the criminal justice system.

They're here (in the criminal justice system), they're queer, get used to it

Just as the criminal justice curriculum has begun to recognize that visible minorities have multi-dimensional experiences, it must also reveal the experiences of the LGBT community as they really occur – within multiple contexts. It is not enough to mention the LGBT community only when we discuss hate crimes (though this is an important topic and I will give you some ideas for addressing it). While many LGBT individuals do face the threat of physical violence, and we should make this clear to our students, we must also prepare our students to recognize, appreciate, and understand the unique issues that the LGBT community faces within each of the major components of the criminal justice system (law enforcement, the court system, and corrections) as employees, victims, and offenders. Including LGBT issues in all components of the criminal justice curriculum is particularly important in light of the evidence that criminal justice majors tend to hold more negative attitudes towards the LGBT community than their peers in other disciplines (Ventura, et al., 2004; Cannon, 2005; Brinson, et al.,

2011) and that criminal justice programs generally lack any focus on LGBT issues at all (Cannon and Dirks-Linhorst, 2006).

Cannon's (2005) study of 1,055 undergraduate students at four different universities, for example, found that criminal justice majors hold more negative attitudes towards gays and lesbians than their peers in other majors. He also found that students who had taken courses that specifically address LGBT issues had "significantly more positive attitudes toward gay men than those who had not" taken such a class (Cannon, 2005, p.235), which is why the sections that follow will offer specific active learning techniques to introduce and/or further explore LGBT issues in law enforcement, corrections, and courts. While the possibilities for making the invisible visible are endless, I hope to provide you a few concrete ideas that will inspire you to develop your own activities.

LGBT issues in law enforcement

Given the research on the attitudes of criminal justice majors, it should come as no surprise that several studies have revealed anti-gay sentiment and behavior among law enforcement officers (e.g., Bernstein and Kostelac, 2002; Wolff and Cokely, 2007; Lyons, et al., 2008) and that LGBT officers struggle with negotiating their identities at work (Miller, Forest, and Jurik, 2003). To address both of these issues simultaneously requires activities that center around the "do's and don'ts" of appropriately interacting with LGBT citizens and colleagues. I have several ideas to suggest for doing this.

The truth of the matter is that, whether they realize it or not, law enforcement officers will most certainly come into contact with LGBT offenders and victims. While an offender's sexuality may not be directly related or relevant to their offense (except, perhaps, in the case of prostitution), there is a chance that someone's sexuality may be directly related or relevant to their victimization, which is why I tend to focus on interaction with LGBT victims (before offenders) when I teach these issues. A victim's sexuality is most likely to be an issue that officers have to be cognizant of in cases of rape and intimate partner violence, so the following activities require students to think about how police officers can best interact with LGBT rape victims.

A review of 75 quantitative studies about sexual assault victimization among LGB individuals suggests that LGB individuals may be at a much greater risk for sexual assault victimization than the general population (Rothman, et al., 2011). Even though sexual assault is one of the most underreported crimes, police officers should nonetheless be prepared to interact with all victims in a compassionate and respectful manner. The rape of Brandon Teena is an excellent case study for broaching this topic.

Brandon Teena was a transgender teenager from Lincoln, Nebraska. Born female, Brandon identified as male and faced years of teasing and bullying from other kids. Eventually Brandon fled Lincoln to start life over in Falls City, Nebraska, where he introduced himself as male and began acquiring friends and dating a young woman named Lana. Those who have heard Brandon's name know him as the victim of a vicious hate crime (a triple murder) committed by Lana's ex-boyfriend, John Lotter, and his friend Tom Nissen. Brandon's brutal murder became the focus of an award-winning (albeit somewhat inaccurate) Hollywood film starring Hillary Swank called *Boys Don't Cry*. I do not doubt that Brandon's murder generally (and the Hollywood film more specifically) are the foundations for many discussions about hate crimes in criminal justice classrooms. Though his murder was a classic example of a hate crime (but not legally a hate crime in most states), it is actually Brandon's experience as a rape victim that I focus on in class.

As those who are familiar with Brandon's case know, he was murdered not only because of Tom and John's extreme outrage at learning that Brandon was biologically female, but also because Brandon had reported to the police after both of them raped him in the back seat of a car. When he reported the rape to authorities, Brandon was victimized a second time by an incredibly homophobic police department. When interviewed by Sheriff Laux about the assault Brandon was asked invasive and irrelevant questions, such as why he sometimes wore a sock in his pants (which he was not wearing at the time of the rape) and "why do you run around with girls, instead of guys, being you are a girl yourself?" Sheriff Laux also asked Brandon why he thought his rapists did not fondle him, saying "I can't believe that if he pulled your pants down and you are a female that he didn't stick his hand in you or his finger in you." At one point the sheriff actually referred to the rape as getting "poked" and asked what happened after John "got a spread of you." In one of the most humiliating moments of the interview Brandon was asked if he "worked it up" for his rapists. Not surprisingly, Laux did not immediately arrest Lotter and Nissen, despite a written statement, which is why they had the opportunity to murder Brandon and two other people.

This interview can be heard in the excellent documentary film *The Brandon Teena Story*, which is available to watch in its entirety or in parts for free online. Once you show the film in class or assign it as out-of-class viewing, I suggest preparing to spend some time "de-briefing" about the film. Because it is a documentary and the footage is real, this film tends to emotionally affect students in a way that *Boys Don't Cry* cannot. It is incredibly powerful and some students, particularly those who have been raped or who identify as LGBT, have very visceral reactions that need to be discussed.

The interview between Sheriff Laux and Brandon provides a backdrop for several activities, and can be supplemented with relevant readings (e.g., Bernstein and Kostelac, 2002; Wolff and Cokely, 2007; Lyons, et al., 2008). One idea would be to engage students in role play activities whereby they demonstrate what the interview *should* have been like for Brandon. This, of course, requires students to think about not only how to interact with LGBT victims, but all victims. You could do this in class or have students videotape their interviews.

Another angle to approach this from is ethics in policing. Have students form Citizen Review Panels (or act as the state Supreme Court if you want to use this case in a courts class), "review" the case, and decide what (if any) sanction Sheriff Laux or the Richardson County Sheriff's Office should face. In this activity you might want to form groups prior to showing the film or interview and use that as part of the "evidence" that the panel must review. You can then have panels compare their decisions and discuss how they came to their conclusions, which can then be explored in the context of actual decisions that were made in relation to the case. Sheriff Laux was eventually found negligent by the Nebraska Supreme Court and Brandon's mother was awarded $81,000 (Brandon v. Richardson County, 2001). The court's final decision can be found on the Lambda Legal website, which is listed in the appendix.

These activities (and/or those used to "lift the veil") can lay the groundwork for a more intense project requiring groups of students to develop their own "sensitivity" training for law enforcement agencies. To be done properly this project should require students to engage and apply the literature on police/citizen interaction and LGBT officers, so that they can address both of those issues in their trainings. The final product could be a PowerPoint presentation and a detailed outline of how they would elaborate on the PowerPoint bullets. Depending on the quality of the final product, you could have students provide the best training to campus or local law enforcement agencies. This is an excellent way to incorporate service learning into your class and for your students to make an impact in their community.

LGBT issues in the court system

I actually find that the issue of hate crimes against LGBT individuals fits best in a broader discussion about the prosecutor's discretion in charging defendants. As of this writing, all but five[8] U.S. states have some form of hate crime legislation which offer prosecutors a chance to pursue additional charges against offenders whose violent or destructive acts were motivated by their hatred for some demographic characteristic (e.g., race) represented by their victim(s). What many people do not realize is that only thirty-one of the states that have passed hate crime legislation included sexual orientation in doing so, and even fewer (13) include both sexual orientation and gender identity. These omissions provide you with another interesting issue to focus on before you even broach the topic of prosecutor discretion. In particular, the failure to include sexual orientation and gender identity in hate crime legislation provides the foundation for a lesson on the limitations of the data provided in the Uniform Crime Report (UCR) by the Federal Bureau of Investigation (FBI).

Just as with other crimes, law enforcement agencies are not required to report hate crimes to the FBI and, of course, if they did report hate crimes to the FBI they would only be reporting those acts that were legally considered hate crimes in their state. I would recommend spending time in class visiting and exploring the FBI's data on hate crimes (or assigning the task as homework if you do not have internet access in your classroom) and discussing how the limitations of the data may be causing us to grossly underestimate hate crimes (particularly those against LGBT individuals). Despite the fact that the FBI data does not paint the whole picture, it does suggest that 1,293 (or 20.8 percent) of the hate crimes that occurred in 2011 were motivated by the victim's sexual orientation and that almost 60 percent of those crimes were committed against gay males (FBI, 2011).

After reviewing the information that we have about hate crimes (and exposing the limitations of that information), you can engage your students in a "what would you do?" type activity that requires students to interpret and apply the legislation in their own state,[9] as if they were the prosecutor in a criminal case. Provide your students with the hate crime law specific to your state (or, better yet, require them to find it themselves outside of class) and then present your students with several potential cases that *may* be considered a hate crime. Their task, of course, will be to decide if they will charge the defendant with a hate crime, based on the parameters of the law. You can present these cases in a variety of ways but I suggest using real cases (as their "real life" outcomes make for excellent post-activity discussion) and I also suggest avoiding cases that students are likely to be familiar with.

One way to present the cases is to create "case files" that include detailed information about the crimes – this is an excellent approach if you are the creative type. However if, like myself, you find yourself short on time I suggest using two of the cases from the 1997 film *Licensed to Kill*, which is a documentary about men who have been convicted of murders presumably inspired by their hatred for homosexuals. Though all of the cases are excellent examples of potential hate crimes, I focus on the cases of Donald Aldrich and Kenneth Jr. French. I chose these cases because, based on nearly every state hate crime law that includes sexual orientation, Aldrich could be charged with a hate crime and French[10] likely could not. While Aldrich lured a gay man from a park, shot him nine times and then freely admitted he shot him because he was gay, French shot four people in a restaurant while he was supposedly "blacked out" from having too much to drink. While French was admittedly homophobic, none of his victims were known to be gay (by him or anyone else), and the only reason he was presumably included in the film is because during the commission of the crime he was screaming about "showing Clinton to let gays in the army." Having a case like French's demonstrates to the students just how much power the prosecutor has, how significant discretion is, how important clarity in the law is, and how complicated it can be to work within the confines of the law. If you choose to use these cases as well, profiles of the men can be found at the website for the production company (DeepFocus), which is included in the appendix. I print the profiles to accompany the four clips that I show from the film – two that detail the crimes and two that are interviews of the convicted men.

What I like about this particular activity and I think is essential to covering hate crimes in the criminal justice classroom is that it forces us to move beyond the spectacle of hate crimes. Hate crimes account for some of the most brutal crimes in American history (e.g., the murder of Matthew Shepard), but it is not enough to teach these cases to our students only to point out how bloody they are and hope that it will disgust or frighten our students into empathy. Today's students are constantly surrounded by violent imagery and come to us from high schools where homophobia is so rampant that we have had to create an entire anti-bullying movement in hopes of reducing suicide among LGBTQ teens. Our students are keenly aware that hate crimes exist and even more aware of the homophobia behind them, which is why we need to go a step beyond simple exposure to discussing these issues in detailed relation to how the criminal justice system does and should respond to them.

LGBT issues in corrections

The corrections classroom is perhaps the trickiest place to talk about LGBT issues, largely because consensual sodomy does occur between heterosexual men and women in prison and, for some reason, this issue tends to bring a lot of homophobia to the surface in a classroom discussion. I have heard some of the most offensive and downright false statements when the issue of gay sex in prison has come up in my class (e.g., "It's a known fact that gay men don't use condoms anyway, so why give them out in prison?" or "If you have sex with a man, you're definitely a queer"). As a lesbian it is incredibly difficult to bite my tongue, but I do so knowing that this is an excellent opportunity for a teachable moment – particularly to discuss that sexuality is more than just sex. Students easily accept this if you "turn the tables" on them. For example, ask them if having sex with a man because there were no women left on earth would make Ellen DeGeneres straight – their immediate answer is "no." End of discussion.

Sex between sexually deprived and consenting adults is, in my view, not worthy of much discussion, so I incorporate LGBT issues in other ways. One topic that has increasing relevance in the corrections classroom is the treatment of transgender inmates. Now, be forewarned, this topic also has the potential to bring out the worst in people – not surprising, given the transphobia that is rampant in our media, such as when Fox's Bill O'Reilly and Megyn Kelly mocked a transsexual inmate named Michelle Kosilek, who was granted gender reassignment surgery by the state of Massachusetts while she was incarcerated. The January 2013 on-air banter was denounced by gay rights groups, but did not catch any attention from mainstream media, no doubt because of the general lack of concern the American public has for both inmates and transgender individuals. Thus, it is very important to "lift the veil" by teaching LGBT issues more generally before raising controversial issues in corrections.

It is likely that transgender individuals come into contact with the criminal justice system at greater rates than non-transgender people

> because they are more likely to be victims of violent crime, because they are more likely to be on the street due to homelessness and/or being unwelcome at home, because their circumstances often force them to work in the underground economy, and even because many face harassment and arrest simply because they are out in public while being transgender. Some transgender women report that police profile them as sex workers and arrest them for solicitation without cause; this is referred to as "Walking While Transgender."
>
> *(Grant, et al., 2011, p.158)*

Thus, it is very important that our students are exposed to the transgender experience before they become employed in the field of criminal justice.

In a survey of 6,450 transgender and gender non-conforming individuals, Grant, et al. (2011) found that 37 percent of those who had been incarcerated reported harassment by correctional officers, 35 percent reported harassment by other inmates, 16 percent reported experiencing physical abuse and 15 percent reported sexual assaults. Not surprisingly, these are higher than the rates for gender conforming individuals, and African American transgender individuals reported the highest rates of abuse while incarcerated. This information, along with an upsurge in lawsuits involving incarcerated transgender inmates and Los Angeles' recent decision to house transgender inmates separately while awaiting arraignment, provides the opportunity for exploring inmate classification and its consequences.

In most cases transgender inmates are classified by their genitalia, regardless of whether or not they are taking hormones or have had breast augmentation, or they are segregated from other inmates. The former is problematic because it ignores the inmate's risk of victimization and the latter is problematic because of the cruel nature of segregating someone for the potential poor behavior of others. In addition to the issue of classification there is the issue of whether or not the state should pay for the sex reassignment surgery (SRS) of transsexual inmates. For addressing both issues I recommend strategies similar to those above. The 2006 documentary film *Cruel and Unusual* can help humanize transgender inmates and cases like Michelle Kosilek's can be used as case studies[11] for answering the question, "what are we obligated to provide to transsexual inmates?"

Part of the key to posing this question to students is to give them specific roles within the criminal justice system. From their position as a citizen, and especially as a taxpayer, their gut reaction is probably not to care at all what happens to transgender inmates, but our job is to prepare them to be professionals that make evidence-based decisions. If we put students in the role of the warden, for example, and describe to them the roles and responsibilities of a warden (e.g., legal liability for the safety of inmates), then they are forced to look at the consequences of key criminal justice decisions that may conflict with their personal opinions.

Another way to challenge the preconceived notions of students is to approach the issue of mental health care in prison. Before even mentioning transgender issues, do a module on mental health issues and incarceration in general. All of the available data on incarceration shows us that mental health is a serious issue both behind bars and upon reentry, and the evidence clearly suggests that mental health care in prison is essential to prison security and successful community reintegration. After presenting this information to your students, it is almost inevitable that they will react affirmatively if you ask them whether or not mental health care should be provided in prison. Then, of course, you turn the tables by asking them whether or not transsexual individuals should be given hormones and/or SRS while incarcerated. When they say no (which I assure you is quite likely), you point out that gender identity disorder (recently relabeled gender dysphoria) is considered to be a mental illness by the American Psychiatric Association. If our belief is that mental illness should be treated in prison, then there are only three conclusions that we can come to (any of which may be correct): either we have an obligation to provide psychiatric care (including medically necessary procedures) to transsexual inmates, *or* transsexualism should not be classified as a mental illness, *or* we believe that some mental illnesses deserve treatment while others do not (and thus a criteria must be outlined). Whatever the conclusion is, you have just opened the can of worms for an exercise in critical thinking.

No, that's not why you hired the lesbian

It should go without saying, but so should most of what I have written here, so let me be explicit – just as racial minorities should not be the only scholars to teach about racial disparity in criminal justice, sexual minorities should not be the only scholars teaching about LGBT issues. The truth is that if a student who holds racist beliefs hears about racism in criminal justice from his or her Black professor it is likely to go in one ear and out the other, considered to be an exaggeration, self-serving, or complaining. The same is true of homophobic students who only hear about the issues raised here by their LGBT faculty. With that said, I think my students gain a lot from coming to respect and appreciate an authority figure that they know is a sexual minority, but part of that respect and appreciation they have learned because it is modeled by my heterosexual colleagues.

In addition to being taught by all faculty, LGBT issues must be infused throughout the curriculum and not relegated to some "special topic section" in the syllabus. While some LGBT issues warrant their own time and space (and can even warrant their own class), we must do with sexual minorities what we have done with racial minorities in our curriculum. As previously mentioned, we now discuss race in relation to everything in criminal justice – it is no longer a "special topic" but an integral part of all of the things we cover in our classes. So, for example, if you use the Brandon Teena activity I suggested, consider doing it as part of a larger lesson about police ethics or rape – doing so sends the message to students that LGBT issues connect to all of the issues we face within the criminal justice system.

Conclusion

We can only hope that Clinton's speech was a sign that the fight for LGBT equality is again being revitalized. Perhaps the passion and determination that sparked the Stonewall uprising is bubbling up to the surface again and maybe, just maybe, this is the turning point and the beginning of yet another journey in our quest for true equality in America. In his 2013 inauguration speech the most visible minority of this generation, President Barack Obama, reminded us that "Our journey is not complete until our gay brothers and sisters are treated like anyone else under the law. For if we are truly created equal, then surely the love we commit to one another must be equal as well." As teachers of justice we must continue to equip our students with the tools that they will need to be successful working within a system where someday there might truly be "justice for all," hopefully because of the work we will inspire them to do and because they are the righteous people that we have helped them to become.

Appendix

Imagine you are a heterosexual[12]

The following exercise is based upon the Guided Imagery developed by Brian McNaught (www.brian-mcnaught.com) and can be adapted to fit nearly every audience. For example, I change the ending of the story depending on my specific goal. Below I offer two possible endings to the story – the first I use in the classroom when I want to teach my students about LGB issues in policing or when I am specifically training police officers on how to interact with the LGB community, and the second I use when I want to address a broader audience or range of issues. How I present the story depends on the resources I have – if I have none, I simply ask students to close their eyes and listen and if I have access to technology (which is preferable) I show a slideshow of images that correspond with the story as I tell it. As many students are "visual" learners I find this strategy to be most effective.

For the next few minutes, I would like you to imagine that you are a heterosexual. In fact, imagine that you were born a heterosexual. I want you to think about what it would be like to be born a heterosexual, but imagine that you are a heterosexual living in a world that is homosexist. In this world, most people believe that homosexuality is the normal, acceptable, and appropriate sexuality. In this world, the judges are gay, the doctors are gay, the majority of television characters are gay, the police officers are gay, the priests are gay, and even your parents are gay. In this world, the popular belief is that heterosexuals are bad, because the majority of child molesters are heterosexual, the majority of rapists are heterosexual, and most heterosexual relationships don't last, so they are considered unsacred. In this world, homosexuals are given the exclusive right to adoption, because it is assumed that they really want children and not just to breed them. A homosexual, after all, never has a child by accident. Imagine what it is like to be a heterosexual in this world.

When you are a child, you start to notice that there is something different about you. When two women come on tv, your sisters get excited because they are lesbians, and when two men come on television your brothers hoot and holler because they are gay. But you don't get excited. In fact, you don't understand why your brothers and sisters want to be with someone of the same sex … the idea of touching someone of the same sex completely grosses you out … instead you get excited when someone of the opposite sex comes on television. You wonder if you should say something. Your family will love you no matter what, right? You decide to tell your family but before you can say anything your father makes a "breeder" joke at the dinner table and you decide that "coming out" wouldn't be a good idea. After all, you desperately want your family to love and accept you. Anyways, it's a few more years before you have to worry about finding someone to love, so you figure you might as well keep it inside.

When you enter high school and all of your friends start to date you begin to worry that you might really be a heterosexual, because you're still attracted to people of the opposite sex. Prom comes and all of your friends and siblings ask people of the same sex to go with them. They are very excited and plan for months. You don't want to be singled out so you ask someone of the same sex to go with you, too. When the night finally comes everyone is laughing and having a great time and dancing together. You put on your best smile and dance with your date, but deep down it just doesn't feel right. You really wish you could be there with a date of the opposite sex, but you pretend you feel the same way everyone else does. It's a good thing you do, too, because one of your rebellious classmates brought an opposite-sex date and got told they had to leave before they caused a disturbance. As they walk out the door your friends make comments about those "breeders who always have to shove it in your face that they're so proud to be hetero!" It wasn't easy hiding who you were and feeling ashamed about who you really might be, but you manage to make it to graduation and you decide to go to college. You're going to go to [insert your university] so you can be close to your family who you love dearly. You're going to make them proud by being the first in your family to go to college.

At this point, take a break from the story and ask students: what is life like in this world so far? How do you feel? Do you feel that other people have things that you don't and can do things that you can't? Use this as an opportunity to define and give some examples of heterosexual privilege. Then, continue with the story ...

So, you're off to [your university]. You notice that there is a lot of gay pride on campus. It seems like almost everything is related to gay relationships. In fact, the school even has a "Miss" and "Mrs." (your university) and every group on campus crowns a gay or transgender couple to represent them. You see some people on campus that you think might be heterosexual (after all, they dress like the heterosexual comedy characters on TV), but none of them actually tell you they're straight. One of your classmates tells you that your science teacher is heterosexual, but all the students and even some of the other faculty call her a "breeder" behind her back. Finally, after your whole fresh-man year goes by you meet someone who is brave enough to tell you that they, like you, are a heterosexual. You are so relieved that you finally have someone to talk to, and even though others on campus start to suspect that you're straight and give you disgusted looks when you are with your new friend, you don't care … pretty soon you get used to the looks and you even get brave enough to "come out" to some of your homosexual classmates. They ask you questions like "When did you realize you were straight?" and say things like "Maybe you just haven't been with the right person yet." These words are hurtful but you try to be gracious because you don't want anyone to hate you.

One night your new straight friend offers to take you to a hetero-sexual bar. All you've heard about straight bars is that they're nothing but a meat market for people to hook up, but you're curious so you decide to go. You stand outside for a few minutes, debating on whether or not you should go in. When you realize that someone you know might see you standing outside of a straight bar, you dash inside. You are amazed at what you see! Men and women are dancing toge-ther … and enjoying themselves … and some of them are from (your university)! You get a drink and stand around uncomfortably until someone (of the opposite sex!) finally asks you to dance. You dance all night and finally meet a group of friends who go to your school who are just like you.

Ending #1: During the school week you go to class and try to keep a low profile. You still don't come out to many people because you don't want to get into some long political or religious debate about heterosexuality or wake up to find anti-heterosexual graffiti around campus or, worse yet, get beat up. Every weekend, though, you are happy … you meet up with your group of heterosexual friends at the club and even start secretly dating members of the opposite sex. One night after the club your small group of friends return to the dorm and start to party. You're laughing and drinking and having a great time, and eventually you drink yourself into a stupor. But when you wake up, you realize something horrible has happened. Your body feels different and you realize that you've had sex – sex you don't remember, sex you can't recall consenting to – you're pretty sure you've been raped by someone of the opposite sex, by a heterosexual. What do you do? Do you go to the police? What factors affect your decision?

Ending #2: You start to date someone, but you both keep it a secret out of fear. During the school week you go to class and try to keep a low profile. You still don't come out to many people or display affection with your partner in public because you don't want to get into some long political or religious debate about heterosexuality or wake up to find anti-heterosexual graffiti around campus or, worse yet, get hurt. You date your new partner for the rest of your Freshman year and are lucky enough to get a dorm room with them in your Sophomore year (since everyone on campus is presumed to be gay, same sex roommates are not allowed and every room has a male and a female). You're still keeping your relationship pretty secret, so as far as most people know your roommate is simply your really good friend. One day you're walking through campus to class and a friend stops you and says, "Hey – aren't you so and so's best friend?" (So and so is your partner). When you say yes, they tell you that your partner, your first love, fell ill in the middle of class and they were rushed to Student Health Services. They tell you it doesn't look good and they might be sent to the local hospital. Your first instinct is to rush to their side, but then you start to worry. Will the gay doctors and nurses send you away? If they find out that you're a couple will they treat your partner badly or not treat them at all because they're a heterosexual? What if they tell other faculty and staff that you're straight? That you're one of "those" people? What do you do? Who do you go to?

Websites for teaching LGBT issues

Human Rights Campaign: www.hrc.org
Movement Advancement Project: www.lgbtmap.org
Federal Bureau of Investigation: www.fbi.gov
National Gay and Lesbian Task Force: http://www.thetaskforce.org/
Lamda Legal: www.lambdalegal.org

Films for teaching LGBT issues (* indicates documentary films)

⋆*8: The Mormon Proposition* (2010)
A Girl Like Me: The Gwen Araujo Story (2006)
⋆*Boys Don't Cry* (1999)
⋆*Cruel and Unusual* (2006)
⋆*Licensed to Kill* (1997)
Philadelphia (1993)
The Brandon Teena Story (1998)
⋆*The Celluloid Closet* (1995)
The Laramie Project (2002)
The Matthew Shepard Story (2002)

Notes

1 Queer is both a political statement disavowing binary definitions of gender and sexuality and a blanket term used to encompass all LGBTIA people. The Q can also stand for Questioning, to include especially young people who are exploring their sexuality.
2 Intersex is a blanket term covering multiple medical conditions that result in ambiguous genitalia that does not fit the "standard" of male or female sex organs.
3 An ally is a non-LGBTQI person who supports and advocates for the equal treatment of all, regardless of gender or sexual orientation.
4 I have actually found this to be the most powerful version of this exercise, and this is how I always do it if the technology is available. It takes a while to prepare, but you can in fact find some very interesting images on the web that complement the story (e.g., a "no breeders allowed" symbol, images of same-sex police officers holding hands, etc.). I've recently adapted the exercise to an online course by adding timed slide/image advancement and audio to a PowerPoint presentation, which can be done with basic PowerPoint software so long as you have a microphone on your computer.
5 The heterosexual privilege list has been dubbed "Unpacking the Invisible Knapsack II" on several websites.
6 Since the Supreme Court decision to overturn the 1996 Defense of Marriage Act, which denied married gay couples the federal benefits afforded to heterosexual couples, eight more states have legalized gay marriage (for a total of 16).
7 A 2012 ruling by the Equal Employment Opportunity Commission ensures that transgender and gender non-conforming individuals are federally protected under Title VII.

8 Arkansas, Georgia, Indiana, South Carolina, Wyoming
9 If, like myself, your state does not include sexual orientation or gender identity in its hate crime statute, I simply take the opportunity to discuss the problematic nature of that and then proceed with the activity as if they live in a more progressive state.
10 I also use the French case because it occurred in Fayetteville, NC, where most of my students are from, and it allows for an important discussion about homophobia and military ethos (as French was in the Army, like many of my students). The case occurred in 1993, so very few of my students know of the case.
11 A simple Google search for "transgender inmates" will yield you several recent lawsuits involving the rights of transgender inmates.
12 Reproduced with kind permission from Brian McNaught.

Bibliography

Bernstein, M. and Kostelac, C., 2002. Lavender and blue: Attitudes about homosexuality and behavior toward lesbian and gay men among police officers. *Journal of Contemporary Criminal Justice*, 18(3), pp.302–28.

Bonilla-Silva, E., 2006. *Racism without racists: Color blind racism and the persistence of racial inequality in the United States*, Lanham, MD: Rowman and Littlefield Publishers, Inc.

Brinson, J., Denby, R., Crowther, A. and Brunton, H., 2011. College students' views of gays and lesbians: A case for a moral exclusion framework. *Journal of Human Services*, 31(1), pp.51–70.

Cannon, K.D., 2005. "Ain't no faggot gonna rob me!": Anti-gay attitudes of criminal justice undergraduate majors. *Journal of Criminal Justice Education*, 16(2), pp.226–43.

Cannon, K.D. and Dirks-Linhorst, P.A., 2006. How will they understand if we don't teach them? The status of criminal justice education on gay and lesbian issues. *Journal of Criminal Justice Education*, 17(2), pp.262–78.

Federal Bureau of Investigation, 2011. *Hate crime statistics, 2011*. [online] Available at: <http://www.fbi.gov/about-us/cjis/ucr/hate-crime/2011/narratives/incid ents-and-offenses> [Accessed 8 April 2013].

Fradella, H.F., Owen, S.S. and Burke, T.W., 2009. Integrating gay, lesbian, bisexual, and transgender issues into the undergraduate criminal justice curriculum. *Journal of Criminal Justice Education*, 20(2), pp.127–56.

Grant, J.M., Mottet, L.A., Tanis, J., Harrison, J., Herman, J.L. and Keisling, M., 2011. *Injustice at every turn: A report of the national transgender discrimination survey*. Washington: National Center for Transgender Equality and National Gay and Lesbian Task Force.

Lenning, E., 2009. Moving beyond the binary: Exploring the dimensions of gender presentation and orientation. *International Journal of Social Inquiry*, 2(2), pp.39–54.

Lyons, P.M., DeValve, M. and Garner, T.L., 2008. Texas police chiefs' attitudes toward gay and lesbian police officers. *Police Quarterly*, 11(1), pp.102–17.

McIntosh, P., 1989. White privilege: Unpacking the invisible knapsack. *Peace and Freedom Magazine*, July/August, pp.10–12.

Miller, S.L., Forest, K.B. and Jurik, N.C., 2003. Diversity in blue: Lesbian and gay police officers in a masculine occupation. *Men & Masculinities*, 5(4), pp.355–85.

Rich, A., 1980. Compulsory heterosexuality and lesbian existence. *Signs: Journal of Women in Culture and Society*, 5, pp.631–60.

Rothman, E.F., Exner, D. and Baughman, A.L., 2011. The prevalence of sexual assault against people who identify as gay, lesbian, or bisexual in the United States: A systematic review. *Trauma, Violence & Abuse*, 12(2), pp.55–66.

Rubin, G., 1984. Thinking sex: Notes for a radical theory of the politics of sexuality. In: C.S. Vance, ed. 1984. *Pleasure and danger: Exploring female sexuality*. Boston: Routledge. pp.267–319.

Ventura, L.A., Lambert, E.G., Bryant, M. and Pasupuleti, S., 2004. Differences in attitudes toward gays and lesbians among criminal justice and non-criminal justice majors. *American Journal of Criminal Justice*, 28(2), pp.165–80.

Wolff, K.B. and Cokely, C.L., 2007. "To protect and to serve?": An exploration of police conduct in relation to the gay, lesbian, bisexual, and transgender community. *Sexuality & Culture*, 11, pp.1–23.

6

FILLING THE VOID

Classroom strategies for teaching about crimes of the powerful

Elizabeth A. Bradshaw

Contemporary students of criminology and criminal justice are missing a comprehensive understanding of social class and its relationship to crime. Historically, within the United States there has been a lack of class consciousness amongst the general population, giving way to the belief that America is a "classless society." Compounding this misnomer, the mainstream media overwhelmingly provides coverage of crimes committed by the poor and working classes, while failing to recognize the social harm perpetrated by people in positions of power such as government and corporate officials. Perhaps most at fault for the continued obfuscation of crime and social harm, the discipline of criminology on the whole has almost exclusively focused on "street" crimes while ignoring white-collar crime, corporate crime, state crime and state-corporate crime (Wright and Friedrichs, 1991; Lynch, et al., 2004; Rothe and Ross, 2008). Taken together, these trends have left students and the general public with the mistaken impression that the most harmful activities in society are committed by the poor and working classes. Based on this false premise criminal justice officials have invested immense resources to target crime in the streets, while allowing crime in the suites to run rampant.

Despite the growing bodies of literature documenting crimes committed by the wealthy and powerful, the criminological discipline has been reluctant to grant serious attention to the social harm perpetrated by members of the upper class. This chapter begins by demonstrating the scarcity of teaching and research on crimes of the powerful and stresses the importance of providing students with a comprehensive understanding of white-collar crimes. Moreover, this chapter seeks to provide readers with a brief overview of the available literature on white-collar crimes (including corporate crime, state crime, and state-corporate crime), and sources for further resources on the topics. Finally, practical suggestions for course activities to introduce students to the relationship between social class and crime are provided.

Criminological resistance to crimes of the powerful

As Reiman and Leighton (2013, p.65) point out, the criminal justice system is not an objective reflection of the most dangerous activities in society, but rather functions as a "carnival mirror" that magnifies the threat of street crime while obscuring other harmful behaviors. The disparities in treatment between the poor and the wealthy that occur throughout the justice system take place *"after most of the dangerous acts of the well-to-do have been excluded from the definition of crime itself"* (p.106). Restricting the label of crime to those acts committed by the poor leaves the public and students with a skewed understanding of the real harms in society.

Despite the resulting economic, physical, and environmental harms, the criminal activity of the upper class has been marginalized in the criminological discourse. Although the concept of white-collar crime was introduced by Edwin Sutherland in the 1940s, criminological research and teaching on the topic did not begin to develop until the 1970s (Wright and Friedrichs, 1991, p.95). For example, it was not until after 1972 that corporate crime and the problems it caused appear within social problems textbooks (Clinard and Yeager, 1980). In reflection of the public sentiment in society more generally, the labeling, conflict, and radical movements within sociology during the 1960s and 1970s helped draw attention to the growing research into crimes of the powerful. Nonetheless, since the introduction of white-collar crimes, criminal justice education has consistently failed to integrate both textbooks and curriculum on crimes of the powerful (Wright and Friedrichs, 1991; Lynch, et al., 2004; Rothe and Ross, 2007). While some criminologists continued to examine these types of crimes, "it is possible to conclude that little changed in criminology since Sutherland first implored criminologists to pay greater attention to the issue of white-collar crime over sixty years ago ... " (Lynch, et al., 2004, p.396). Through its underrepresentation in the traditional peer reviewed academic journals of the discipline, in its absence from introductory textbooks in criminology and criminal justice, and in the scarcity of curricula within university Ph.D. programs in criminology and criminal justice, the study of corporate crimes has been diminished (Lynch, et al., 2004).

State crime has similarly been marginalized within criminology. Most universities do not require nor regularly offer courses on state crime (Ross and Rothe, 2007). Additionally, state crime is also under-represented in introductory textbooks on crime and criminal justice, and the few textbooks that do address state criminality are insufficient (Rothe and Ross, 2008). Frequently, references to state crimes within textbooks often present examples that lack historical context and are outdated such as Watergate or the Iran-Contra scandal. Therefore, instructors who are given the opportunity to teach a course on state crime are often forced to cobble together their own teaching materials, which can pose additional challenges for those unfamiliar with the topic (Ross and Rothe, 2007).

Yet despite these barriers, the demand for courses on state crime is on the rise. Even in the face of "the constraints of curriculum, practitioner-oriented goals of students, and the focus on mainstream street crime – there appears to be a growing interest among students in taking a class on state crime. Simultaneously, there appears to be a growing acceptance of and interest in crimes of the state by criminologists" (Ross and Rothe, 2007, p.472). It seems that while the demand for courses on state crime is growing, there continues to be a deficiency in university level courses to address it. It is therefore imperative that educators attempt to integrate these topics into a range of criminology and criminal justice courses in an effort to shift the public debate on class and crime.

White-collar crimes: corporate, state, and state-corporate

When Edwin Sutherland articulated the concept of white-collar crime in 1940, the samples examined by criminologists at the time were almost exclusively comprised of the poor, and failed to include the harmful behavior of business and professional men (Sutherland, 1940). Sutherland attributed the source of this disparity to the biased application of law to upper class criminals compared to the poor. White-collar crimes, Sutherland observed, were often not defined as violations of criminal law, but were instead classified as violations of regulatory law. A radical shift from the street crimes being studied by most criminologists of the time, white-collar crime highlighted both the importance of high social status and occupational setting to the study of criminality.

One of the earliest identified sub-categories of white-collar crime is crimes committed by corporations. Corporate crime can be defined as "offenses committed by corporate officials for their corporation and the offenses of the corporation itself" (Clinard and Quinney, 1973, p.188). Crimes committed by governments (state crime) are also considered white-collar crimes, involving people of high social status during the course of their occupation. State crime includes illegal acts committed by state officials in pursuit of their jobs as state representatives, such as the state's complicity in piracy, smuggling, assassinations, criminal conspiracies, and violating laws that limit their activities (e.g., spying on citizens) (Chambliss, 1989, p.184).

As the literature on white-collar crimes has illustrated, people in positions of power such as government and corporate officials are able to manipulate the law to define activities typically committed by the poor as criminal, while neglecting to classify their own socially harmful behavior as crime. Thus, state criminality also encompasses socially injurious behavior that would be considered deviant and invoke public censure if discovered, even if the action is not necessarily classified by law as illegal. In many cases, state organizational deviance takes the form of seemingly legitimate state operations and organizations which become entangled with illegal ones, thereby making it difficult to easily categorize "legal" and "illegal" state crimes (Green and Ward, 2000).

State-corporate crime involves the collaboration of government and business entities that cause illegal or socially injurious behavior, resulting from the policies of one or more institutions of political governance or economic production or distribution (Michalowski and Kramer, 2006, p.21). State-initiated corporate crime occurs when corporate actors engage in organizational deviance and the direction of government institutions. One classic example of state-initiated corporate crime is the 1986 space shuttle *Challenger* explosion which resulted in the death of seven crew members (Kramer, 1992). The disaster resulted after NASA (a government agency) put pressure on Morton Thiokol (a corporation) to launch despite concerns raised by engineers about the safety of the O-rings on the shuttle. State-facilitated corporate crime, on the other hand, results from the failure of government institutions to effectively regulate the deviant business practices of corporations (Michalowski and Kramer, 2006). An example of state-facilitated corporate crime is the U.S. government's facilitation of climate change by failing to regulate the fossil fuel industry (Lynch, et al., 2010; Kramer and Michalowski, 2012).

Strategies for teaching about crimes of the powerful

With the deficiency of literature on corporate crime, state crime, and state-corporate crime within the academic institution itself, it perhaps is not surprising that the public perception of crime remains confined to the actions of the poor. If students of criminology and criminal justice are not exposed to the academic research on crimes committed by the powerful, then they are left with an inaccurate understanding of the social harm occurring around the world today. Students must be shown that societal definitions of crime are shaped by the criminal law which often excludes harm committed by governments and corporations. Demonstrating that crime and criminality is not an objective phenomenon, but rather is defined through the process of law creation, can help students to understand how crime is socially constructed. Furthermore, teaching future justice system leaders about white-collar crime increases the likelihood that these types of crimes will be given higher priority (Wright and Friedrichs, 1991, p.211). Therefore, teachers must employ creative classroom activities to unveil the relationship between power, wealth, and crime.

Stratification monopoly activity

Although unconventional learning activities may fail to replicate real-life experience, evoke negative emotion, and are difficult to grade, they may improve student engagement and participation. "Stratification Monopoly" is an excellent class activity to demonstrate societal inequality and begin establishing connections between class and crime. To help students experience different levels of social stratification, Coghlan and Huggins (2004) provide a template for using a modified version of the board game Monopoly in introductory sociology and social problems courses. Students are assigned to groups of five or six, depending on the class size and availability of boards. Each of the groups' five players selects a game piece, which correspond to the five income quintiles in the U.S. (as identified by the Census Bureau). From the beginning, property is given to the top two quintiles, and stratified salaries are given out for "passing GO." Whoever selects the top quintile token is also given the power to be banker, and becomes the defaulting authority on all unclear rules. Once the game is over, students are asked to tally their total ending assets and compare them to their starting assets. Afterwards, students are assigned a reflection activity asking them to relate the assigned readings to the activity (Coghlan and Huggins, 2004). Following the reflection, a class discussion takes place on the experience of the game, and how it relates to social class, mobility, laws, and crime.

The exercise is easily adaptable to different types and sizes of courses (see Coghlan and Huggins, 2004 for sample assignments). The game can easily be altered for a course on deviance or criminal justice. For example,

> Modifications in the "deviance" version include creating legal and illegal opportunity cards (with consequences) for players to acquire additional income in the game, specific guidelines on the exchange of loans and gifts among players, and instructions for the sale of property by individual players.
>
> *(Coghlan and Huggins, 2004, p.179)*

Although I have not tried the deviance modifications suggested by the authors, I have incorporated the activity into sections of up to 65 students in *Social Problems, Introduction to Criminal Justice,* and *Inequalities in Justice Processes: Race, Class and Gender.* Even without tailoring the exercise to illustrate deviance, the activity provides students with an interactive means of understanding how the structures of society (i.e., "the rules of the game") differentially shape individual life chances. Ultimately, the effectiveness of the exercise hinges on the instructor's ability to facilitate meaningful discussion that helps students relate the experience to the course concepts.

Interestingly, many students begin to embody their assigned roles in the game. I have noticed that the "rich" students often become louder and more aggressive, while the "poorest" students become frustrated and disengage from the game entirely. Echoing this observation, recent research in the discipline of psychology has similarly used the Stratification Monopoly exercise to demonstrate how people who feel wealthy (even within the context of the game) become greedier, less empathetic, and behave more rudely to other players (PBS Newshour, 2013; Piff, et al., 2012). In addition, PBS Newshour (2013) has a useful video clip *Exploring the Psychology of Wealth, 'Pernicious' Effects of Economic Inequality* that can be used to further engage students in a discussion on wealth, inequality, and empathy.

Films on state and corporate criminality

Incorporating more popular culture, music, and films is another pedagogical tool used to illustrate to students the relationship between social class and crime. Teaching about state crime through route lecture and endless statistics cannot convey the experience of those victimized by the state. Films, on the other hand, have the ability to more immediately and convincingly portray an instance of state crime that students can identify with (Rothe and Ross, 2007, p.332). For instance, communicating the horror of genocide and other state atrocities to relatively privileged college students is not an easy task (Day, et al., 2003). When teaching students about genocide, "There is a risk that the victims of such extreme violence may seem distant and unreal, their experiences unimaginable, and thus incomprehensible. A failure to convey the realities of individual experience can make the whole topic seem abstract and unreal" (Day, et al., 2003, p.10). The struggle of connecting abstract law and policy to the concrete harm and suffering experienced by the victims of state and corporate wrongdoing is a challenge to teaching about such complex topics.

Many students find it difficult to understand the processes by which governments and corporations collaborate to produce laws that harm members of the poor and working classes while benefiting wealthy businesses. If teachers are unable to clarify these relationships, then students can be left with the impression that crimes committed by governments and corporations are merely "conspiracy theories." I have used a number of films in the classroom to expose students to crimes committed by people in positions of power. Produced by Moyers and Company, the documentary *The United States of ALEC* (2012) provides a concrete example of exactly how government and corporate officials work together to craft legislation on a wide range of criminal justice issues. The hour-long film details the operations of the American Leg-islative Exchange Council (ALEC) which brings together corporations and state legislators to draft "Model Legislation" that representatives can then introduce as their own back home. Since ALEC has produced Model Legislation for mandatory minimum sentences, privatization of prisons, Stand Your Ground Laws, and Arizona's SB1070 criminalizing undocumented immigrants, there are ample applicable contemporary criminal justice issues that can be brought into the classroom.

After showing the video and facilitating class discussion, one activity that helps students to explore these laws and their origins is to organize students into groups and provide each group with a different example of ALEC Model Legislation related to criminal justice. Students are then asked to consider how each piece of Model Legislation might benefit vested corporate interests, as well as what indirect and direct effects it might have on the criminal justice system as a whole (e.g., increasing prison sentences and incarceration rates). The website *ALEC Exposed* (The Center for Media and Democracy, 2012) provides copies of many different Model Legislation on a range of issues, especially in the section on "Guns, Prisons, Crime and Immigration." Most students have never heard of ALEC (nor have many professors), and many are surprised – and even angered – that such a formal organization exists to facilitate greater corporate involvement in politics. Furthermore, a number of students have even reported that ALEC was the most interesting and/or shocking thing they learned about throughout the course. By providing clear examples of how government and corporate actors collaborate to produce laws that benefit the rich over the poor, students are better able to understand and critically analyze the vested interests involved in law formation and its impact on contemporary justice issues.

Another video which is useful for illustrating the complex relationship between individual and organizational deviance is the HBO documentary *Ghosts of Abu Ghraib* (2007), which examines the 2004 Abu Ghraib prisoner abuse and torture scandal. The film interviews many of the soldiers involved in the abuse and critically questions how they came to participate in such inhumane and degrading actions. Many of the soldiers interviewed faced disciplinary actions, and showed remorse for what they had done, even though they were "just following orders" of superiors. Moreover, the documentary also explores how policies formed by top-level Bush administration officials permitted torture and created an institutional environment in which it was acceptable. In this regard, the film does an excellent job of demonstrating how government policy issued by high-level officials translates into the harmful actions of soldiers on the ground.

While it is clear to students that the prisoners were victimized, many had difficulty viewing the soldiers who took part in the abuse as victimized by government policies that cultivated an environment that encouraged abuse. The majority of students felt as though each individual soldier was solely responsible for his or her own actions at Abu Ghraib and should be held accountable accordingly. One student felt as though the video demonized the soldiers and was personally offended since a family member was also serving overseas. Although my goal in showing the video was to encourage students to consider how law and policy shapes the actions of individuals who are obeying rules from superiors, it seems as though many students missed this point. In the future I plan to spend more time discussing exactly how organizational policies affect an individual's actions. Moreover, before showing the video, I plan to preface it by spending more time discussing how top Bush administration officials crafted policy that not only justified the use of torture, but encouraged soldiers to take such actions.

Challenging students' notions about the War on Drugs, the film *American Drug War: The Last White Hope* (2007) explores drug policy and questions who benefits from it. The film considers the effects of drug use in society, including alcohol and prescriptions drugs, and critically examines how government policy has exacerbated the problem through criminalization. Moreover, the film explores allegations that the Central Intelligence Agency, with the tacit approval of the Reagan administration, was involved in trafficking cocaine into inner-city communities during the 1980s as a means of raising funds for the anti-communist Nicaraguan Contras. While some are skeptical of such claims, *American Drug War* encourages students to move beyond paradigms that criminalize drug users and consider the differential effects of drug policy on the rich versus the poor. Although students have criticized the video for being too long, it provides a thorough analysis of drug use in America and considers alternative models of decriminalization that students often support.

Alongside this video, I conduct an activity in which groups of students are given the current Drug Enforcement Administration's (DEA) Drug Schedules and the criteria for each classification. Next, students are asked to re-classify the Drug Schedule based on the harm each drug poses to individuals and society, and provide a justification for altering the classification. I then have students report back to the class as a whole what changes were made and why. Student responses often reflect the social acceptance of certain kinds of drug such as alcohol, marijuana, and prescription drugs. Many students argue for removing marijuana from the DEA's Schedule entirely, while some think that it should be in the least harmful category (although it remains in the most harmful category). Other students think that alcohol should be included in the most harmful category. Some categorize drugs by method of use, stating that any drug that is injected should be treated more harshly due to its threats to public health. Overall, this activity encourages students to move beyond drug policies that criminalize the poor and imagine alternatives that are geared towards harm reduction.

Newsmaking criminology

Once students are able to see beyond public misconceptions of crime and have developed a solid understanding of the relationship between social class, harm, law, and crime, then it is possible to engage them in the process of changing the public discourse. "Newsmaking criminology refers to criminologists' conscious efforts and activities in interpreting, influencing, or shaping the presentation of 'newsworthy' items about crime and justice" (Barak, 1988, p.566). This practice urges criminologists to publicly establish themselves as experts on crime, and to take part in policy formation surrounding justice and defining harm, crime, offenders, and victims. Recognizing that objective newsmaking does not exist, Barak (p.585) calls upon critical and progressive criminologists "to participate in the social construction of crime and crime control as a means of bringing about social change and social justice." Introducing students to concepts of harm and justice that highlight the disparity between crime in the street and crime in the suite is the first step towards addressing crimes of the powerful.

While it is imperative for criminologists to participate in newsmaking criminology, it is similarly important to teach students of crime and justice to do the same. As students leave the classroom and embark on a multiplicity of criminal justice careers, they must feel empowered to challenge traditional definitions of criminality that frame the poor and working classes as the greatest source of harm in society. If more students of critical criminology become involved in the public discourse on social class and crime, then crimes committed by the wealthy and powerful will get sorely deserved media attention. Given the skills to make empirical connections between their educational training and contemporary examples of state and corporate deviance, students of critical criminology have the potential to alter the public perception of crime and social class both through their personal and professional actions.

Conclusions

Public and media recognition of white-collar criminality as a legitimate source of societal harm ultimately depends on the ability of criminologists to influence the discourse on such topics. To effectively teach about the relationship between social class and harm, it is necessary to move beyond the confines of traditional notions of crime and criminal justice and introduce students to corporate, state, and state-corporate criminality. Despite the lack of university courses, representation in textbooks, and media attention to government and corporate crimes, student demand for courses on these topics persists (Ross and Rothe, 2007).

While it is quintessential for intellectuals to partake in newsmaking criminology, it is essential to encourage students of criminology and criminal justice to engage in these public debates as well. Even though white-collar crime has been slow to garner attention, recent social movements against state and corporate power – such as the Occupy movements in the U.S. and globally, as well as renewed allegations of invasive government surveillance – have provided fertile ground for teaching about crimes of the powerful. Contemporary examples of state and corporate criminality are plentiful, and though there may be substantial student interest in these areas, criminology needs more critical educators willing to introduce students to these complex topics.

Appendix

Recommended films

American drug war: The last white hope. 2007. (War on Drugs)

Capitalism: A love story. 2009. (Financial crisis and other harms caused by capitalism)

Enron: The smartest guys in the room. 2005. (Corporate Crime)

Gasland. 2009. (State-corporate environment crime and hydraulic fracturing)

Ghosts of Abu Ghraib. 2007. (Abuse and Torture)

Hotel Rwanda. 2004. (Genocide)

Iraq for sale: The war profiteers. 2006. (Crimes of occupation)

Prisons for profit. 2006. (Private prisons)

The big fix. 2011. (State-corporate environmental crime and the BP Gulf of Mexico oil spill)

The corporation. 2003. (Corporate crime)

The flaw. 2011. (2008 Financial collapse and foreclosure crisis)

The house I live in. 2012. (War on Drugs)

The invisible war. 2012. (Sexual assault in the US military)

The Madoff Affair. 2009. (White-collar crime)

The one percent. 2006. (Wealth inequality)

The road to Guantanamo. 2006. (Torture)

The United States of ALEC. 2012. (Corporate Control of Legislative Process)

Why we fight. 2005. (Crimes of aggression, military-industrial complex)

Recommended readings

Barak, G., Leighton, P. and Flavin, J., 2010. *Class, race, gender and crime*. 3rd ed. Lanham, Maryland: Rowman and Littlefield.

Chambliss, W., Michalowski, R. and Kramer, R. eds., 2010. *State crime in the global age*. Portland, OR: Willan Publishing.

Friedrichs, D.O., 2010. *Trusted criminals: White collar crime in contemporary society*. 4th ed. Belmont, CA: Thomson Wadsworth.

Reiman, J. and Leighton, P., 2013. *The rich get richer and the poor get prison: Ideology, class, and criminal justice*. 10th ed. Boston: Pearson.

Rothe, D. and Mullins, C., 2011. *State crime: Current perspectives*. Piscataway, NJ: Rutgers University Press.

Bibliography

American drug war: The last white hope. 2007. [DVD] *American drug war: The last white hope*. Studio City, CA: Sacred Cow Productions.

Barak, G., 1988. Newsmaking criminology: Reflections on the media, intellectuals, and crime. *Justice Quarterly*, 5(4), pp.566–587.

Chambliss, W., 1989. State-organized crime – The American Society of Criminology, 1988 Presidential Address. *Criminology*, 27(2), pp.183–208.

Clinard, M.B. and Quinney, R., 1973. *Criminal behavior systems: A typology*. New York: Holt, Rinehart & Winston.

Clinard, M. and Yeager, P., 1980. *Corporate crime*. New York: Free Press.

Coghlan, C.L. and Huggins, D.W., 2004. "That's not fair!" A simulation exercise in social stratification and structural inequality. *Teaching Sociology*, 32, pp.177–87.

Day, L.E., Vandiver, M. and Janikowski, W.R., 2003. Teaching the ultimate crime: Genocide and international law in the criminal justice curriculum. *Journal of Criminal Justice Education*, 14(1), pp.119–31.

Ghosts of Abu Ghraib. 2007. [DVD] *Ghosts of Abu Ghraib.* New York City: Home Box Office (HBO).

Green, P. and Ward, T., 2000. State crime, human rights, and the limits of criminology. *Social Justice,* 27(1), pp.101–15.

Kramer, R., 1992. The space shuttle *Challenger* explosion: A case study of state-corporate crime. In: K. Schlegel and D. Weisburd, eds. *White collar crime reconsidered.* Boston: Northwestern University Press, pp.214–43

Kramer, R. and Michalowski, R., 2012. Is global warming a state-corporate crime? In: R. White, ed. *Climate change, crime and criminology.* New York: Springer, pp.71–88.

Lynch, M., Burns, R. and Stretesky, P., 2010. Global warming and state corporate crime: The politicization of global warming under the Bush administration. *Crime, Law, Social Change,* 54, pp.213–39.

Lynch, M., McGurrin, D. and Fenwick, M., 2004. Disappearing act: The representation of corporate crime research in criminological literature. *Journal of Criminal Justice,* 32, pp.389–98.

Michalowski, R. and Kramer, R. eds., 2006. *State-corporate crime: Wrongdoing at the intersection of business & government.* New Brunswick: Rutgers University Press.

PBS Newshour, 2013. *Exploring the psychology of wealth, "pernicious" effects of economic inequality.* 21 July 2013. Available at: <http://www.pbs.org/newshour/bb/business/jan-june13/makingsense_06–21.html> [Accessed 1 November 2013].

Piff, P., Stancato, D., Cote, S., Mendoza-Denton, R. and Keltner, D., 2012. Higher social class predicts increased unethical behavior. *Proceedings of the National Academy of Sciences,* 109(11), pp.4086–91.

Reiman, J. and Leighton, P., 2013. *The rich get richer and the poor get prison: Ideology, class, and criminal justice.* 10th ed. Boston: Pearson.

Rothe, D. and Ross, J.I., 2007. Lights, camera, state crime. *Journal of Criminal Justice and Popular Culture,* 14(4), pp.330–43.

——, 2008. The marginalization of state crime in introductory textbooks on criminology. *Critical Sociology,* 34, pp.741–52.

Ross, J.I. and Rothe, D., 2007. Swimming upstream: Teaching state crime to students at American universities. *Journal of Criminal Justice Education,* 18(3), pp.460–75.

Sutherland, E.H., 1940. White-collar criminality. *American Sociological Review,* 5(1), pp.1–12.

The Center for Media and Democracy, 2012. *ALEC exposed.* 28 September 2012. Available at: <http://www.alecexposed.org/wiki/ALEC_Exposed> [Accessed 1 November 2013].

Moyers & Company, 2012. *The United States of ALEC.* Available at: <http://bill moyers.com/episode/full-show-united-states-of-alec-a-follow-up> [Accessed 1 November 2013].

Wright, R.A. and Friedrichs, D.O., 1991. White-collar crime in the criminal justice curriculum. *Journal of Criminal Justice Education,* 2(1), pp.95–121.

7

WOMEN ARE MORE THAN VICTIMS

Gender, crime and the criminal justice system[1]

Walter S. DeKeseredy

Everything we teach is transmitted to students within a specific political economic context. Criminology is less gender-blind than it was 20 years ago and there has been a recent explosion of feminist contributions to the field (see Renzetti, 2013). This is not to say, though, that it is much easier now to teach about the gendered nature of crime and social control than it was in the past, especially if you publicly identify yourself as a feminist. What Faludi (1991, p.xix) stated nearly 23 years ago still holds true today: "[I]f fear and loathing of feminism is a sort of perpetual viral condition in our culture, it is not always in an acute stage; its symptoms subside and resurface periodically." For example, from the mid to late 1990s, every time I lectured on various types of male violence against women in intimate relationships, I would hear at least 10 students publicly say in class that they "don't want to hear this stuff." Many others would glare at me, while at least 10 would quickly leave the classroom at the start of my lecture. An unknown, but I assume large, number of my female colleagues experienced more intense "anti-feminist classroom swarming" when they discussed the same topics (Menzies and Chunn, 1991). Today, more students are willing to learn about gender violence behind closed doors, but those that do not, resist by using more sophisticated methods, one of which is citing journalistic and scholarly materials claiming that females are becoming increasingly violent and masculinized (Chesney-Lind and Irwin, 2008).

Many instructors also confront this claim in courses on women and crime and those on women and the criminal justice system. As well, numerous students, mostly males, warmly embrace the stereotype of women in conflict with the law as "having it easy" or routinely "getting off the hook" when, in reality, more females are subject to criminal justice intervention than ever before and girls receive harsher punishments for status offenses than do boys (Dragiewicz, 2012; Pasko and Chesney-Lind, 2012). The main objective of this chapter is twofold: (1) to describe these and some other key challenges faced by feminists who teach about gender, crime, and criminal justice; and (2) to describe some effective ways of sensitizing students to realities of women in conflict with the law.

"But women do it too!" moral panics in the classroom

You have likely heard some of your colleagues say that when gender is brought up in the context of crime and criminal justice, it is generally assumed that men are primarily offenders and women are mainly victims. There is ample evidence to support this notion. Despite all of the good things men have contributed to the world, much of what is bad on this planet, from genocide to terrorism, and including interpersonal violence, is essentially the product of men and some of their masculinities (Bowker, 1998; DeKeseredy and Schwartz, 2005). A large social science literature shows that males, especially those who are patriarchal, also perpetuate the bulk of violence in intimate heterosexual relationships throughout the world (DeKeseredy, 2011a; DeKeseredy and Schwartz, 2013).

Similarly, men "have a virtual monopoly" on the commission of crimes of the powerful, such as price-fixing and the illegal dumping of toxic waste (Messerschmidt, 1997; Messerschmidt and Tomsen, 2012). And, one would be hard-pressed to find more than a handful of women involved in acts of state terrorism.[2] Additionally, how often do we hear about women participating in mass killings such as the one in Newtown, Connecticut on December 14, 2012? How many women took part in the plot to fly planes into the World Trade Center and the

Pentagon on September 11, 2001? At the risk of belaboring the issue, the most important point to consider is that a variety of data sets show that men's involvement in most types of violent crime exceeds that of women (DeKeseredy, 2011a; Dragiewicz and DeKeseredy, 2012).

Still, *some* women commit violent crime and this problem should not be ignored. While criminology has been slow to examine women's use of violence (Boots and Wareham, 2013), the media have not dragged their heels and the bulk of the information generated by the press caused a moral panic about "unruly women" and "the new bad girl" (Faith, 1993; Chesney-Lind and Irwin, 2008). Hollywood movies (e.g., *Mean Girls*) and academics (e.g., Garbarino, 2006), too, contribute to distorted perceptions of women's use of violence (DeKeseredy, 2010). This is one of the key reasons why the mantra "But women do it too" is endemic to courses about girls, women, and crime, especially those that focus on male-to-female victimization in ongoing relationships and during and after separation/divorce.

The concept of the moral panic was developed by Stanley Cohen (1980) to describe a situation in which a condition, episode, person, or a group of persons come to be defined as a threat to society. The objects of moral panics are usually people. The media, together with criminal justice officials, some social scientists, and other "experts" jumped on the bandwagon to transform women and girls who violate a myriad of patriarchal gender norms in the U.S., Canada, and in other countries into "folk devils." A folk devil is "a socially constructed stereotypical carrier of significant social harm" (Ellis, 1987, p.199). As well, while girls' violence has, in reality, been decreasing, arrests for their violence have steeply increased (Brown, et al., 2013). Also, media portrayals of adult females who engage in violence as "irrational," "wicked," or "demonic" negatively "affect their punishment in the criminal justice system and perhaps breed rationalization of violence against women" (Grabe, et al., 2006, p.158).

This moral panic is not a function of ignorance or the inability to obtain reliable crime data. Rather, it is a prime example of "patriarchy reasserted" (Dragiewicz, 2008). True, North American college/university campuses have undergone significant progressive changes since the 1960s. Even so, women's inroads into classrooms, administrative jobs, tenure-track positions, student governments, and so on threaten many men's perceptions of their masculinity. The "but women do it too" statement, then, is a technique that a sizeable portion of these male students use to assert their perceived superiority and dominance and to keep women in their proper place (DeKeseredy, et al., 2007; DeKeseredy, 2009a).

I find that claims of "but women do it too" are usually more common in courses on domestic violence and violence against women. A growing number of women also make this assertion and some of my female students brag in class that they have hit their current or former male partners. Unfortunately, the few that do this are viewed by some men in the class as reliable data that can be generalized to the entire female population. Let us also not forget that there is an increasing number of right-wing women in schools today who are "virulently antifeminist"(Bacchetta and Power, 2002), and in every first-, second-, and third-year course I have ever taught, very few female students raise their hands when I ask all of the women in the class to do so if they define themselves as feminists. Most of the other women, I assume, do not dislike feminists or feminism, but fear being stigmatized and marginalized by their male peers. Needless to say, too, that homophobia comes into play with these women because of right-wing media stereotypes of feminists as being lesbian. Fear of violence is another determinant, given that DeKeseredy, et al. (2007) found that the Canadian female undergraduates in their sample who were most likely to be the targets of hate-motivated sexual assault were those who publicly identified themselves as feminist.

Universities/colleges are not as safe as commonly assumed. Ironically, while such institutions contribute to the advancement of learning and broadening young minds, DeKeseredy, et al.'s (2007) study of campus hate crime supports Ehrlich's (1999) claim that postsecondary institutions are showing dramatic intolerance, as evidenced by ongoing, even escalating rates of racial, ethnic, and gender harassment. Furthermore, although there may be a strong international emphasis on gender violence as a hate crime and as a violation of women's human rights (Stark, 2007; DeKeseredy, 2009a), in North America, gender as a status category continues to take "a detour on the road to hate crime policy acceptance but is traveling the road nonetheless" (McPhail, 2003, p.275).

Proving that gender matters

Millions of people from various walks of life, including the vast majority of undergraduate students and many faculty, confuse gender with sex. These two concepts are related but are not the same (Daly and Chesney-Lind, 1988). Following Flavin and Artz (2013, p.11), gender refers to "the socially defined expectations, characteristics, attributes, roles, responsibilities, activities and practices that constitute masculinity, femininity, gender identity, and gender expressions."

There are, to be sure, consistent sex differences in crime that are heavily influenced by dominant gender norms (Schur, 1984; Dragiewicz, 2009). Note, too, that men and women may commit the same crimes, but for different reasons. For example, men steal as a means of "doing masculinity" and tend to "pinch" goods like stereos and tools, items that are not necessary for their survival (Messerschmidt, 1993; DeKeseredy, 2000; Chesney-Lind and Pasko, 2013). On the other hand, women steal items that are lower in value but are useful to them as mothers, homemakers, or for feminine appearances, such as clothing, groceries, and makeup. They also write bad checks mainly to get these items. Likewise, most women who defraud the government do so because they and their children cannot afford to live on minimal welfare payments or wages accumulated from "pink ghetto" work (Barker, 2009a; Morash and Yingling, 2012).

To give another example, a growing number of highly problematic studies consistently show that men and women commit equal rates of violence in intimate heterosexual relationships. These studies typically use some rendition of the Conflict Tactics Scales (CTS), originally developed by Murray Straus (1979), and they are aggressively used by anti-feminists to support the claim that women are as violent as men (Dragiewicz and DeKeseredy, 2012). For feminists who have used the CTS or who have examined data gleaned by them, it may seem painfully obvious but worth stating again nonetheless: the CTS ignores the contexts, meanings, and motives of both men's and women's violence (DeKeseredy, 2011a). Unless researchers can accurately determine why women use physical violence against men, it is important to inform students that it is irresponsible to contend, as psychologist Donald Dutton (2006, p.ix) does, that "in Canada and the United States, women use violence in intimate relationships to the same extent as men, for the same reasons, and with largely the same results."

To reach these conclusions, proponents of sexual symmetry artificially narrow the definition of violence between intimates to obscure injurious behaviors that display marked sexual asymmetry, such as sexual assault, strangulation, separation assault, stalking, and homicide. Rather than an unacceptable or hysterical broadening of the definition of violence, these behaviors are commonly part of abused women's experiences (DeKeseredy and Schwartz, 2009; Dragiewicz and DeKeseredy, 2012). Like others who contend that women are as violent as men (e.g., Straus, 2011), Dutton and his allies downplay research on these forms of violence. Moreover, they pay little attention to differentiating between defensive and offensive forms of violence between intimates, a courtesy we extend to victims of other crimes (DeKeseredy and Dragiewicz, 2007).

To make claims about the symmetry of violence between intimate partners, one must also conflate sex and gender. Discussions of prevalence that rely on the variables "male" and "female" cannot tell us much about gender, the socially constructed and normative set of meanings attached to these categories. This distinction is one of the primary contributions of feminist perspectives to the social sciences (Dragiewicz, 2012). Research that asks perpetrators and survivors about the nature of violence between intimates finds that both say much about gender. For example, rural violent men talk about threats to their masculinity when their intimate female partners leave or try to leave them (DeKeseredy, et al., 2007; DeKeseredy and Schwartz, 2013), whereas women talk about the normative expectations that abusers use to justify their violence (DeKeseredy and Dragiewicz, 2007).

Proving that gender matters is increasingly becoming a challenge in the classroom and elsewhere because of the anti-feminist backlash and the fact that feminist criminology continues to be marginalized at many institutions of higher learning (Dragiewicz, 2012). Furthermore, even if one repeatedly focuses on the importance of gender, she or he is likely to be outnumbered by colleagues in his or her department who are preoccupied with only focusing on men and boys when relaying information to students about victimization, offending, and the criminal justice system (Renzetti, et al., 2013). This imbalance helps promote students' resistance to a feminist understanding of women's experiences with crime and societal reactions to it.

Confronting misunderstandings about feminism

A substantial number of people mock those who refer to themselves as feminist. Heavily influenced by the media, religious groups, and conservative politicians, these people equate feminism with hating men, not shaving one's legs, going braless, being gay or lesbian, and being pro-choice (DeKeseredy and Schwartz, 1996). Of course, some feminists fit into one or more of these categories; however, it is no surprise to readers of this anthology that many men and women are feminists. Actually, I define myself as a feminist man. I and other feminists are united by a deep desire to eliminate all forms of gender inequality.

It is a challenge to sensitize students to the fact that the goal of feminist scholars who study women in conflict with the law is "not to push men out so as to pull women in, but rather to gender the study of crime and justice" (Renzetti, 1993, p.232). It is also a challenge to get students to recognize that it is misleading to paint all feminists with the same brush. There is no unitary feminist perspective in criminology and students have difficulties understanding that there are at least 12 brands of feminism with major debates within each brand (Maidment, 2006; Renzetti, 2013). For the purpose of this chapter, I offer Kathleen Daly and Meda Chesney-Lind's (1988, p.502) definition, which refers to feminism as "a set of theories about women's oppression and a set of strategies for change."

Other variants of critical criminology (e.g., left realism, Marxism, and postmodernism) are also met with sharp resistance by numerous students, most of whom are conservative and are deeply uncomfortable with a pedagogical approach that requires them to think critically about the society in which they live.[3] Will feminist teachers face even more resistance in this current climate? This is an empirical question that can only be answered empirically. Nevertheless, the aforementioned backlash is alive and well and is not likely to recede in the near future.

Equality with a vengeance: women, girls, and the new penal state[4]

Female crime, female victimization, female poverty, and sexist criminal justice practices, such as the reclassification of girl status offenders, are all symptoms of a much larger problem: patriarchy. Many North Americans sharply disagree with this claim and contend that women in the advanced Western world have achieved equality, the call for equity is simply "radical feminist rhetoric" that is divorced from reality, and that women have "made it" (Faludi, 1991). If the "battle has been won," then why are alarming numbers of North American girls and women sexually and physically abused by men and boys?[5] Why are married and cohabiting women still mainly responsible for household chores (Armstrong and Armstrong, 2010)? Further, if women "have made it," why won't, according to a study conducted at Queen's University, Canadian women experience real gender equality until six centuries from now (Brennan, 2012)?

While women are still far from reaching true equality in most major institutions, such as the workplace, the military, and so on, they are starting to obtain it in the criminal justice system. There have been recent dramatic increases in girls' arrests for violent crimes in the U.S., especially those that occur in domestic realms and in schools. Further, due to a lack of gender-specific programs, there have been major increases in the detention and incarceration of girls (Pasko and Chesney-Lind, 2012). Additionally, girls are generally punished more often than boys for minor crimes and for breaching court orders (Alvi, 2009). Moreover, by 2009, the number of women incarcerated in the U.S. increased by 800 percent over the past 30 years, and the number of incarcerated women surpassed that of men over the same time period (West, 2010; Chesney-Lind and Pasko, 2013). These data and similar findings reported elsewhere seriously challenge the chivalry hypothesis, which is the premise that women are treated differently than men by the criminal justice system and that they benefit from the system's paternalistic and protective attitudes (Boritch, 1997).

The increase in the amount of girls and women charged for various crimes is an outcome of more punitive societal reactions to their behaviors heavily fueled by the anti-feminist backlash (Chesney-Lind and

Pasko, 2013). I lived and taught most of my life in Canada and one of the most frequent techniques Canadian students use to support their claim of women "getting off easier" in the criminal justice system is the case of Karla Homolka. How it was reported by journalists (e.g., Pearson, 1997) also led many Canadians to believe that violence among Canadian women and girls is "sharply on the rise" (Chisholm, 1997). In the early 1990s, Homolka, arguably "Canada's most infamous female offender in the latter half of the 20th century" (Barker, 2009a, p.76), and her now ex-husband Paul Bernardo, sexually assaulted and murdered three young women in southern Ontario, one of whom was her sister. To the horror of many Canadians, Homolka struck a plea bargain deal with prosecutors for a reduced sentence of 12 years in prison. This "pact with the devil"[6] received an unprecedented amount of media coverage and continues to be used for political purposes by anti-feminists and supporters of a more punitive Canadian criminal justice system.

Homolka's crimes and the criminal justice system's response to them have shaped Canadians' perceptions of women offenders in general (DeKeseredy, 2000; Barker, 2009a). A key challenge in the classroom, then, is to show that people like her and U.S. female serial killer Aileen Wuornos are not typical offenders. Unfortunately, prior to taking courses on gender and crime, it is fair to assume that most under-graduate students' knowledge of crimes committed by females is based on watching Hollywood movies, which is why many of them perceive women and girls in conflict with the law are masculinized monsters, lesbian villains, incarcerated teenage predators, or pathological killer beauties (Faith, 1993; Holmlund, 1994; Chesney-Lind and Eliason, 2006; DeKeseredy, 2009b).

Related to the problems of trying to portray an accurate picture of what Barker (2009a) refers to as the "typical female offender" and to effectively demonstrate that women do not "get off easier" is the task of challenging students' perceptions of the criminal justice system as being "soft" in general. Consider the U.S., one of the most punitive, yet most violent, countries in the world (Currie, 2009). It continues to experience an "imprisonment binge" (Irwin, 2005), with more than two million people behind bars (DeKeseredy, 2011b). U.S. citizens are locked up four times as often than in the early 1970s and this "mass incarceration" or "new penalism" is racialized (Chesney-Lind, 2007;

Foster and Hagan, 2007). Furthermore, 26 U.S. states and the U.S. federal government have "three-strikes, you're out" sentencing laws. Prisons do little, if anything to reduce the overall crime problem (Reiman and Leighton, 2013), but, buttressed by a large cadre of conservative politicians, journalists, and other "experts," instructors continue to face a critical mass of students who strongly support mass incarceration.

What is to be done?

There are obviously other challenges that instructors face when teaching courses about women, crime, and criminal justice, and it is beyond the scope of this chapter to describe them all. The central point to keep in mind is that there are many effective ways of dealing with the issues covered here and enhancing students' sociological understanding of women in conflict. Obviously, my suggestions constitute just the tip of the iceberg. Furthermore, my ideas and experiences may not match many people's day-to-day realities. As my feminist peers will quickly point out, as a white middle-class man, I have access to resources unobtainable to scores of others and I am relatively immune to anti-feminist classroom swarming. Still, I strongly believe that my recommendations are of some value to my colleagues.

Ask students to be reflexive

Regardless of which criminology class I teach, at the start of my first lecture or seminar, I ask students to raise their hands if they have not committed a crime. Typically, nobody moves. Then, I ask students to explain why they do not have a criminal record and are not behind bars if they have committed a crime or two. The most common response is "I didn't get caught." My inaugural question enables me to challenge the myth that "criminals" are fundamentally different from "non-criminals" and that "everybody does it" (Gabor, 1994; DeKeseredy, 2013a). In women and crime courses, this question also helps me make the point that women in conflict with the law are not distinct from other women (Comack, 1996; Barker, 2009a).

Experts in the field are fully aware, though, that many female offenders have a history of victimization, especially at the hands of men.

Also, for numerous survivors of child abuse and intimate partner violence, crime is the only perceived viable option that allows them to escape from violence (Comack, 1996, 2005; Barker, 2009b). To help students, especially males, understand how violence is an everyday concern for most women, I first present statistics on the extent and distribution of woman abuse in North America. However, numbers are, for many people, little more than abstract clusters of symbols, which students often use to distance themselves from a problem. Further, researchers and instructors frequently deal with those who assert, "You can't believe statistics," especially if these data do not support their opinions. Thus, I always try to influence students to think what it is like for women to constantly live with the fear of male violence.

Following Jackson Katz (2006), I achieve this goal by asking the men in my class to describe the techniques they use to prevent themselves from being raped. At first, none respond; eventually one or two will say something like, "Avoid going to prison." I write this down under the heading "Men." Next, I ask the women to describe their avoidance strategies. A completely different picture emerges. Under the heading "Women," I write down a long list of responses, including avoiding night classes, not walking alone at night, carrying whistles and alarms, calling the campus foot patrol for escorts to the bus or a car, and a host of other preventative measures.

This exercise serves three important functions. First, it shows male students that many women worry about their safety and that their routine activities are governed by a well-founded fear of being attacked by men. Second, many women who thought they were the only ones who worried about being victimized discover that they are not alone. Third, it enables me to ask a question informed by the work of Chesney-Lind and Pasko (2013): "Why do so few women murder, given the alarming amount of violence that North Americans experience in private places?" I then present female homicide statistics showing that the bulk of domestic murders committed by women are "self-help homicides" (Jones, 1994); that is killing the men who sexually assault and beat them. Most, if not all, of my students quickly learn that the bulk of women who kill are not like Aileen Wurnos or Karla Homolka.

Use non-academic texts

Again, it is easy to dismiss statistics. Thus, it is essential for students to see women in conflict with the law through the eyes of real people, and one way of achieving this goal is requiring them to read popular or "trade" books about female offenders' experiences. One powerful, widely read and highly intelligible Canadian book immediately comes to mind: Anne Kershaw and Mary Lasovich's (1991) *Rock-A-Bye Baby: A Death Behind Bars*. It is the story of Marlene Moore who was designated by Mr. Justice Eugene Eswaschuk as "Canada's most dangerous woman." Marlene was routinely physically and sexually assaulted and was nowhere near as dangerous as she was perceived to be by the criminal justice system. In fact, she never harmed anyone as much as she hurt herself. She would slash her body to alleviate emotional pain and she eventually committed suicide at the age of 31 in the Federal Prison for Women in Kingston, Ontario. Books like this one remind students that each statistical data set discussed in my lectures and academic tests is intensely personal and documents women's lived experiences. They also sensitize them to the fact that criminologists are not simply playing a "numbers game" when they collect and disseminate statistics on abuse.

Guest speakers

If trade books add a human dimension to courses, so do guest speakers, especially progressive practitioners who provide services to women in conflict with the law (e.g., parole officers). I always invite guest lecturers to my class because they not only describe real-life pain and stress, but they also discuss the financial, personal, and political problems associated with the front-line struggle to help women and female youth who are in conflict with the law or who are high risk of becoming so. Additionally, service providers can offer students information about how to pursue a career assisting women in conflict with the law. Above all, practitioners help students understand that focusing on women's involvement in crime is much more than a scholarly enterprise and that many women in their own communities suffer in silence with little or no social support.

Electronic technologies

Students spend more time using a computer, iPhone, iPad, or other electronic devices than they do in the classroom. Further, most, if not all, classrooms include computer equipment designed to enhance students' understanding of course material. Thus, instructors should encourage students to use technologies to examine the personal, empirical, and political aspects of the topic and to lead them to discover that learning about, responding to, and preventing female crime are major concerns around the world. For example, organizations such as the Canadian Association of Elizabeth Fry Societies post interesting materials about services and programs available to adult females and youth. Further, Elizabeth Fry Societies across Canada provide "quick facts" about women in conflict with the law on their web sites.[7]

In my own case, increasingly, I use Skype in the classroom to communicate with colleagues in other places who specialize in gender-related issues and to introduce students to people they read about. Most students thoroughly enjoy guest lectures given by my friends and colleagues and a critical mass of students usually follow up on such events by emailing my guest speakers. Unfortunately, institutions of higher learning are spending much less money on bringing in guest speakers than they did in the past but Skype is a highly effective means of overcoming this challenge.

Focus on variations in feminist thought

Given the widespread disdain for feminists and feminist inquiry, it might be easier or less stressful to simply avoid discussing feminism altogether in gender and crime courses. However, such silence only serves to legitimate students' hostility to feminism and indirectly justifies their tendency to paint all feminists with the same brush (Freedman, 2002; DeKeseredy, 2003). To help break down barriers, I suggest beginning your lectures on feminism by citing Claire Renzetti's (1993) statement about the goal of feminist scholars, which was included in a previous section of this chapter. Then emphasize that feminists are not front-line soldiers in the war against men. Rather, they are involved in an ongoing struggle for equality between the sexes. It is also important to stress that many men identify themselves as feminist and are actively involved in a variety of individual and collective efforts to eliminate violence against women and other symptoms of gender inequality. Further, drawing upon sources such as DeKeseredy and Schwartz (2013), Katz (2006), and Funk (2006), provide evidence showing that although many of them may not publicly identify themselves as feminist, millions of male and female allies are currently working around the world for universal recognition of gender equality. This strategy will not make many conservative students more accepting of feminism, but it demonstrates that feminism is "alive and well," and is not regarded as deviant by a sizeable portion of North Americans and residents of other countries.

The next step is to critically review various feminist perspectives on gender and crime. Given time constraints, I usually only discuss the four most widely applied theories: liberal feminism, Marxist feminism, socialist feminism, and radical feminism. On top of highlighting the important contributions made by those who adhere to these schools of thought, this approach tells students that there is more than just one type of feminism and the feminist theoretical literature is characterized by considerable debate. Moreover, to challenge the popular notion that feminist theories are political agendas rather than sophisticated social scientific means of making sense of gender and crime, I summarize empirical tests of feminist perspectives.

Conclusion

Universities and colleges are not simply bastions of liberal thought divorced from the realities of day-to-day life. On the contrary, they are under siege by rabid neoliberalism and the arts and humanities are major targets (DeKeseredy, 2013b). To make matters worse, the anti-feminist backlash described in this chapter and by others (e.g., Dragiewicz, 2011) is turbo-charged, which makes it difficult to promote thinking critically about gender and crime in undergraduate classes. Nevertheless, my feminist colleagues and I will persevere and treat gender as "more than a variable" in all of our courses (Chesney-Lind, 2000). It is also important to remember that we are not alone. The American Society of Criminology's (ASC) Division on Women and Crime and its members offer a warm shelter from the neoliberal storm and provide excellent teaching tips. The same can be said about the ASC's Division on Critical Criminology, another progressive collective that has a large number of members who study and teach about gender and crime. When all is said and done, social support from your peers is arguably the best means of survival in the classroom and in other academic arenas. I know that I cannot do my job without it.

Appendix

Websites for teaching gender and crime issues

Canadian Association of Elizabeth Fry Societies: http://www.eliza bethfry.ca/

National Criminal Justice Reference Service site titled "Women & Girls in the Criminal Justice System": https://www.ncjrs.gov/spotlight/wgcjs/ summary.html

The White House Council on Women and Girls: http://www.white house.gov/administration/eop/cwg/data-on-women

Institute on Women & Criminal Justice's Punitiveness Report: http:// www.wpaonline.org/institute/hardhit/part1.htm

Films for teaching gender and crime issues

Evil Has a Beautiful Face: The Karla Homolka Story (2007)

Flirting with Danger: Power & Choice in Heterosexual Relationships (2013)

Sin by Silence (2009)

Hard Time – Female Offenders (2011)

Aimee's Crossing (2008)

Aileen: Life and Death of a Serial Killer (2003)

Tough Guise (2002)

Girl, Interrupted (2003).

Notes

1 I would like to thank Rebecca Hayes and Kate Luther for their comments and incredible patience.

2 State terrorism is defined here as "the type of governmental abuse and terror perpetrated by traditional dictatorships, from Europe to Central and South America" (Barak, 2003, p.129).

3 See DeKeseredy (2011b) and DeKeseredy and Dragiewicz (2012) for in-depth reviews of the major critical criminological schools of thought.

4 *Equality with a Vengeance* is the title of Molly Dragiewicz's (2011) book on efforts by conservative fathers' rights groups to undermine the 1994 Violence Against Women Act and battered women's shelters and services.

5 See DeKeseredy (2011a), DeKeseredy and Schwartz (2013), and Renzetti, Edleson, and Bergen (2011) for in-depth reviews of the social scientific literature on the extent and distribution of various types of woman abuse in North American intimate relationships.

6 This is the subtitle of Stephen Williams' (2003) book on Karla Homolka.

7 See, for example, http://www.efrytoronto.org/n/sites/default/files/files/Fact_Sheet%202009%20(2).pdf.

Bibliography

Alvi, S., 2009. Female youth in conflict with the law. In: J. Barker, ed. 2008. *Women and the criminal justice system: A Canadian perspective*. Toronto: Emond Montgomery Publications. pp.229–56.

Armstrong, P. and Armstrong, H., 2010. *The double ghetto: Canadian women and their segregated work*. 3rd ed. Toronto: Oxford University Press.

Bacchetta, P. and Power, M., 2002. Introduction. In: P. Bacchetta and M. Power, eds. *Right-wing women: From conservatives to extremists around the world*. London: Routledge. pp.1–15.

Barak, G., 2003. *Violence and nonviolence: Pathways to understanding*. Thousand Oaks, CA: Sage.

Barker, J., 2009a. A "typical" female offender. In: J. Barker ed. *Women in the criminal justice system: A Canadian perspective*. Toronto: Emond Montgomery Publications. Ch. 3.

——, 2009b. Background experiences of women offenders. In: J. Barker ed. *Women in the criminal justice system: A Canadian perspective*, Toronto: Emond Montgomery Publications. Ch.4.

Boots, D.P. and Wareham, J., 2013. A gendered view of violence. In: C.M. Renzetti, S.L. Miller and A.R. Gover, eds. *Routledge international handbook of crime and gender studies*. London: Routledge. pp.163–76.

Boritch, H., 1997. *Fallen women: Female crime and criminal justice in Canada*. Toronto: Nelson.

Bowker, L.H., 1998. Introduction. In: L.H. Bowker, ed. *Masculinities and violence*. Thousand Oaks, CA: Sage. pp.xi–xviii.

Brennan, R.J., 2012. Economic equality for women still centuries off: Parity won't occur until 2593, study shows. *Toronto Star*, 23 May p.A3.

Brown, L.M., Chesney-Lind, M. and Stein, N., 2013. Patriarchy matters: Toward a gendered theory of teen violence. In: M. Chesney-Lind and

L. Pasko, eds. *Girls, women, and crime: Selected readings*. Los Angeles: Sage. pp.21–34.

Canadian Association of Elizabeth Fry Societies, 2013. *Mission statement*. [online] Available at: <http://www.elizabethfry.ca> [Accessed 17 June 2013].

Chesney-Lind, M., 2000. Foreword. In: W.S. DeKeseredy, ed. *Women, crime and the Canadian criminal justice system*. Cincinnati: Anderson. pp.iii–v.

——, 2007. Epilogue: Criminal justice, gender and diversity: A call for passion and public criminology. In: S.L. Miller, ed. *Criminal justice research and practice: Diverse voices from the field*. Boston: Northeastern University Press. pp.210–20.

Chesney-Lind, M. and Eliason, M., 2006. From invisible to incorrigible: The demonization of marginalized women and girls. *Crime, Media, Culture*, 2, pp.29–47.

Chesney-Lind, M. and Irwin, K., 2008. *Beyond bad girls: Gender, violence and hype*. New York: Routledge.

Chesney-Lind, M. and Pasko, L., 2013. *The female offender: Girls, women, and crime*. 3rd ed. Thousand Oaks, CA: Sage.

Chisholm, P., 1997. Bad girls: A brutal B.C. murder sounds an alarm about teenage violence. *MacLeans*, [online] Available at: <http://www.macleans.ca/newsroom120897/cov112897.htm> [Accessed on 3 June 2000].

Cohen, S., 1980. *Folk devils and moral panics*. Oxford, UK: Blackwell.

Comack, E., 1996. *Women in trouble*. Winnipeg: Fernwood.

——, 2005. Coping, resisting, and surviving: Connecting women's law violations to the histories of abuse. In: L.F. Alarid and P. Cromwell, eds. *In her own words: Women offenders' views on crime and victimization*. Los Angeles: Roxbury. pp.33–43.

Currie, E., 2009. *The roots of danger: Violent crime in global perspective*. Upper Saddle River, NJ: Prentice Hall.

Daly, K. and Chesney-Lind, M., 1988. Feminism and criminology. *Justice Quarterly*, 5, pp.497–538.

DeKeseredy, W.S., 2000. *Women, crime and the Canadian criminal justice system*. Cincinnati: Anderson.

——, 2003. The challenge of teaching woman abuse in deviance courses. In: M.D. Schwartz and M.O. Maume, eds. *Teaching the sociology of deviance*, 5th ed. Washington, D.C.: American Sociological Association.

——, 2009a. Male violence against women in North America as hate crime. In: B. Perry, ed. *Hate crimes: The victims of hate crime*. West Port, CT: Praeger. pp.151–72.

——, 2009b. Female crime: Theoretical perspectives. In: J. Barker, ed. *Women and the criminal justice system: A Canadian perspective*. Toronto: Emond Montgomery. Ch.2

——, 2010. Moral panics, violence, and the policing of girls: Reasserting patriarchal control in the new millennium. In: M. Chesney-Lind and N. Jones, eds. *Fighting for girls: New perspectives on gender and violence*. Albany, NY: SUNY Press. pp.241–54.

——, 2011a. *Violence against women: Myths, facts, controversies*. Toronto: University of Toronto Press.

——, 2011b. *Contemporary critical criminology*. London: Routledge.

——, 2013a. The myth that "criminals" are fundamentally different from "non-criminals." In: R.B. Bohm and J. Walker, eds. *Demystifying crime & criminal justice*. 2nd ed, New York: Oxford University Press. Ch.2.

——, 2013b. Welcome to the dark side: Some thoughts on the challenges of being an early progressive scholar. *The Criminologist*, 38, pp.44–45.

DeKeseredy, W.S. and Dragiewicz, M., 2007. Understanding the complexities of feminist perspectives on woman abuse: A commentary on Donald G. Dutton's rethinking domestic violence. *Violence Against Women*, 13, pp.874–84.

——, eds, 2012. *Routledge handbook of critical criminology*. London: Routledge.

DeKeseredy, W.S. and Schwartz, M.D., 1996. *Contemporary criminology*. Belmont, CA: Wadsworth.

——, 2005. Masculinities and interpersonal violence. In: M.S. Kimmel, J. Hearn and R.W. Connell, eds. *Handbook of studies on men and masculinities*. Thousand Oaks, CA: Sage. pp.353–66.

——, 2009. *Dangerous exits: Escaping abusive relationships in rural America*. New Brunswick, NJ: Rutgers University Press.

——, 2013. *Male peer support and violence against women: The history and verification of a theory*. Boston: North Eastern University Press.

DeKeseredy, W.S., Donnermeyer, J.F., Schwartz, M.D., Tunnell, K.D. and Hall, M., 2007. Thinking critical about rural gender relations: Toward a rural masculinity crisis/male peer support model of separation/divorce assault. *Critical Criminology*, 15, pp.295–311.

DeKeseredy, W.S., Perry, B., Pearson-Nelson, B. and Schwartz, M.D., 2007. Sexual assault as hate crime: Results from a Canadian campus survey. Paper presented at the annual meetings of the *American Society of Criminology*, Atlanta, November 2007.

Dragiewicz, M., 2008. Patriarchy reasserted: Fathers' rights and anti-VAWA activism. *Feminist Criminology*, 3, pp.121–44.

——, 2009. Why sex and gender matter in domestic violence research and advocacy. In: E. Stark and E.S. Buzawa, eds. *Violence against women in families and relationships*. Volume 3. Santa Barbara: Praeger. pp.201–15.

——, 2011. *Equality with a vengeance: Men's rights groups, battered women, and antifeminist backlash*. Boston: Northeastern University Press.

——, 2012. Antifeminist backlash and critical criminology. In: W.S. DeKeseredy and M. Dragiewicz, eds. *Routledge handbook of critical criminology*. London: Routledge. pp.280–89.

Dragiewicz, M. and DeKeseredy, W.S., 2012. Claims about women's use of non-fatal force in intimate relationships: A contextual review of the Canadian research. *Violence Against Women*, 18, pp.1008–26.

Dutton, D.G., 2006. *Rethinking domestic violence*. Vancouver. B.C.: University of British Columbia Press.

Ehrlich, H.J., 1999. Campus ethnoviolence. In: F. Pincus and H.J. Ehrlich, eds. *Ethnic conflict*. Boulder, CO: Westview. pp.277–90.

Ellis, D., 1987. *The wrong stuff: An introduction to the sociology of deviance*. Toronto: Macmillan.

Faith, K., 1993. *Unruly women: The politics of confinement and resistance.* Vancouver, B.C.: Press Gang.

Faludi, S., 1991. *Backlash: The undeclared war against American women.* New York: Crown.

Flavin, J. and Artz, L., 2013. Understanding women, gender, and crime: Some historical and international developments. In: C.M. Renzetti, S.L. Miller and A.R. Gover, eds. *Routledge international handbook of crime and gender studies.* London: Routledge. Ch.1.

Foster, H. and Hagan, J., 2007. Incarceration and intergenerational social exclusion. *Social Problems,* 54, pp.399–433.

Freedman, E.B., 2002. *No turning back: The history of feminism and the future of women.* New York: Ballentine.

Funk, R., 2006. *Reaching men: Strategies for preventing sexist attitudes, behaviors, and violence.* Indianapolis: JIST Life.

Gabor, T., 1994. *Everybody does it: Crime by the public.* Toronto: University of Toronto Press.

Garbarino, J., 2006. *See Jane hit: Why girls are growing up more violent and what we can do about it.* New York: Penguin Press.

Grabe, M.E., Trager, K.D., Lear, M. and Rauch, J., 2006. Gender and crime news: A case study test of the chivalry hypothesis. *Mass Communication and Society,* 9, pp.137–63.

Holmlund, C., 1994. A decade of deadly dolls: Hollywood and the woman killer. In: H. Birch, ed. *Moving targets: Women, murder and representation.* Berkeley, CA: University of California Press. pp.127–51.

Irwin, J., 2005. *The warehouse prison: Disposal of the new dangerous class.* Los Angeles: Roxbury.

Jones, A., 1994. *Next time she'll be dead: Battering and how to stop it.* Boston: Beacon.

Katz, J., 2006. *The macho paradox: Why some men hurt women and how all men can help.* Naperville, IL: Sourcebooks.

Kershaw, A. and Lasovich, M., 1991. *Rock-a-bye baby: A death behind bars.* Toronto: McClelland & Stewart.

Maidment, M., 2006. Transgressing boundaries: Feminist perspectives in criminology. In: W.S. DeKeseredy and B. Perry, eds. *Advancing critical criminology.* Lanham, MD: Lexington. pp.43–62.

McPhail, B., 2003. Gender-bias hate crimes: A review. In: B. Perry, ed. *Hate and bias crime: A reader.* New York: Routledge. Ch.19.

Menzies, R. and Chunn, D.E., 1991. Kicking against the pricks: The dilemmas of feminist teaching in criminology. In: B.D. MacLean and D. Milovanovic, eds. *New directions in critical criminology.* Vancouver, B.C.: Collective Press. pp.63–70.

Messerschmidt, J.W., 1993. *Masculinities and crime: Critique and reconceptualization of theory.* Lanham, MD: Roman & Littlefield.

——, 1997. *Crime as structured action: Gender, race, class, and crime in the making.* Thousand Oaks, CA: Sage.

Messerschmidt, J.W. and Tomsen, S., 2012. Masculinities. In: W.S. DeKeseredy and M. Dragiewicz, eds. *Routledge handbook of critical criminology.* London: Routledge. Ch.13.

Morash, M. and Yingling, J., 2012. Adult women in conflict with the law. In: W.S. DeKeseredy and M. Dragiewicz, eds. *Routledge handbook of critical criminology*. London: Routledge. Ch.30.

Pasko, L. and Chesney-Lind, M., 2012. Girls' violence and juvenile justice: A critical examination. In: W.S. DeKeseredy and M. Dragiewicz, eds. *Routledge handbook of critical criminology*. London: Routledge. Ch.19.

Pearson, P., 1997. *When she was bad: Violent women and the myth of innocence.* Toronto: Random House.

Reiman, J. and Leighton, P., 2013. *The rich get richer and the poor get prison.* 10th ed. Boston: Allyn & Bacon.

Renzetti, C.M., 1993. On the margins of the malestream (or, they *still* don't get it, do they?): Feminist analyses in criminal justice education. *Journal of Criminal Justice Education*, 4, pp.219–34.

——, 2013. *Feminist criminology.* London: Routledge.

Renzetti, C.M., Edleson, J.L. and Bergen, R.K., eds., 2011. *Sourcebook on violence against women.* 2nd edn. Thousand Oaks, CA: Sage.

Renzetti, C.M., Miller, S.L. and Gover, A.R., eds., 2013. *Routledge handbook on crime and gender studies.* London: Routledge.

Schur, E., 1984. *Labeling women deviant: Gender, stigma, and social control.* Philadelphia: Temple University Press.

Stark, E., 2007. *Coercive control: How men entrap women in personal life.* New York: Oxford University Press.

Straus, M.A., 1979. Measuring intrafamily conflict and violence: The Conflict Tactics (CT) Scales. *Journal of Marriage and the Family*, 41, pp.75–88.

——, 2011. Gender symmetry and mutuality in perception of clinical-level partner violence: Empirical evidence and implications for prevention and treatment. *Aggression and Violent Behavior*, 16, pp.279–88.

West, H.C., 2010. *Prison inmates at mid-year – Statistical tables.* Washington, D.C.: U.S. Department of Justice.

Williams, S., 2003. *Karla: A pact with the devil.* Toronto: Cantos.

CONCLUSION

All of our chapters illustrate how our dedication to teaching these sensitive topics is rooted in our desire to adequately prepare our students for their work in the criminal justice system, as well as educate them to be social justice minded individuals. As future police officers, victim advocates, lawyers or correctional officers, we want our students to understand the complexities and intersections of gender, race, class and sexuality. For example, each time we hear about racial profiling in the criminal justice system or a case where a police officer engages in victim blaming, we should reflect on how we are teaching our students about these issues. We should question whether we are teaching in a manner that perpetuates or decreases these incidents. Are we effectively teaching our students to recognize their own social location and how that has affected their opportunities? Additionally, are we showing them how our society has created institutionalized "isms" that disproportionately impact certain groups in negative ways? It is our hope that this edited volume provides instructors with the tools to best teach these sensitive topics.

Overarching each chapter in this series is the notion of creating a classroom rapport where students feel comfortable discussing these sensitive topics freely. In that, the authors draw significant attention to our student populations. As we plan our courses, most of us spend our time considering the material we will present and may not devote ample time to considering *who* the students are that will fill our classroom seats. Our classrooms contain victims, offenders and family members or friends of both victims and offenders. Although the authors do not suggest changing course material based on the composition of our courses, they do draw awareness to properly framing and discussing particular topics. Additionally, we must consider our students' backgrounds. Do our students come from communities where prejudice and discrimination is prevalent and accepted? What kind of socialization did they receive regarding gender, race, class and sexuality? These are difficult questions, but if we want our students to have a positive learning experience, we must consider all of these factors as we plan and teach our courses.

Another consideration is to reflect on the stereotypes and prejudice that accompany each topic we teach. For example, if we know students connect being black or poor to criminality, we must come to our classes prepared with ways to turn these comments into teaching moments. Instead of "knee jerk" reactions, we need to have thoughtful and constructive ways to address inflammatory comments. Our tactics in these settings can make or break a class. There are many different approaches illustrated in this book that show us how to respond to our students in ways that clearly address the problematic comment or behavior, but do not make students feel they have been shut out of a class discussion. For many of our students, our classroom may be their first exposure to the social construction of gender or race and we need to provide a safe space for them to explore these topics. We may get tired of continually reframing students' comments or deconstructing a particular issue, but we need to consider the pedagogical importance of these moments in our classrooms. Our ability to do this not only educates our students on the particular material, it also models to them acceptable behavior on a contentious topic. As future employees, whether in the criminal justice system or not, it is beneficial to be able to discuss complex and controversial topics in a calm, educated and thoughtful manner.

Although each of these chapters examined a particular status or issue, we ask you to consider how to teach these topics from an intersectional standpoint. For instance, when teaching about policing, instead of focusing on gender and sexuality separately, think about how they often intersect. In particular, challenge your students to consider how police officers might view and treat a victim of sexual assault if he was male and gay. The suggestions from each of our authors should help to guide you as you navigate the complicated terrain of these sensitive topics.

This volume brought together some of the top criminological inequality scholars, but more importantly passionate teachers. Anyone who reads this volume likely fits into that categorization and will hopefully be inspired by the chapters in this book. However, do not let this book be the end of the conversation. We encourage you to check out the teaching resources from the American Society of Criminology (ASC), the ASC's Division on Women and Crime, and the American Sociological Association (see below). These resources, which include syllabi, assignments, activities, sessions at annual meetings and newsletter teaching tips, are a great place to continue your education on best practices for teaching sensitive topics in criminal justice.

Resources for further reading

American Society of Criminology Teaching Committee, *Teaching tips column*. [online] Available at: <http://www.asc41.com/criminologist. html> [Accessed 5 January 2014].

American Sociological Association, *Teaching resources and innovations library for sociology*. [online] Available at: <http://trails.asanet.org/ Pages/default.aspx> [Accessed 5 January 2014].

Barron, N.G., Grimm, N.M. and Gruber, S., 2006. *Social change in diverse teaching contexts: Touchy subjects and routine practices*. New York: Peter Lang.

Division on Women and Crime Teaching and Pedagogy Committee, 2011. *Teaching resources: Syllabi and assignment collection*. [online] Available at: <http://www.hts.gatech.edu/dwc/images/stories/DWC_syllabi_ 11.pdf > [Accessed 5 January 2014].

Holsinger, K., 2012. *Teaching justice: Solving social justice problems through university education*. Farnham, England: Ashgate.

hooks, b., 2010. *Teaching critical thinking: Practical wisdom*. New York: Routledge.

Kaufman, P., 2006. *Critical pedagogy in the classroom*. 2nd ed. Washington, DC: American Sociological Association.

INDEX